"OFF THE WALL SONNETS" FOR MICHAEL JACKSON

"OFF THE WALL" SONNETS FOR MICHAEL JACKSON

A Memorial Tribute Revisited

FREDERICK MONDERSON

SUMON PUBLISHERS

FREDERICK MONDERSON

"Off the Wall Sonnets" for Michael Jackson Photo. Part of throngs of people who swarmed the Apollo Theater at the Memorial for the deceased musical genius.

SuMon Publishers
PO Box 160586
Brooklyn, New York 11216

ISBN – 978-1-61023-099-5
LCCN - 2026903487

In the **Tribute to Professor George Simmonds**, "Unsung Hero," **Dr. Fred Monderson** sat at the feet of his heroes, Brother X, Michael Carter, Dr. Leonard Jeffries, Elombe Brathe, Dr. Lewis, Prof. George Simmonds, Dr. ben-Jochannan, Sister Camille Yarbrough, among others.

"OFF THE WALL SONNETS" FOR MICHAEL JACKSON

TABLE OF CONTENTS

INTRODUCTION I 9

Thoughts on Michael Jackson

INTRODUCTION II 23

Thoughts on Michael Jackson

1. MICHAEL! A Song of Praise

2. Sonnets, Sentiments of LOVE from the People, His Fans! 42

3. MICHAEL JACKSON – ARCHANGEL 80

4. MICHAEL JACKSON – BELOVED 84

5. The Staple Center Memorial to Michael Jackson on July 7, 2009. 86

+6. BEATING BACK WOLVES AT THE DOOR 93

7. JOE JACKSON 99

8. THE BODY OF WORK (Partial) 102

9. THE MICHAEL JACKSON 103

TIMELINE

10. PRESIDENTS TO PRISONERS SALUTE MICHAEL JACKSON 108
11. EXPRESSING THE VOICE OF THE PEOPLE 111
12. COMMENTATORS ON MICHAEL JACKSON 118
13. VISCERAL CONCERN 121
14 MICHAEL JACKSON IN RETROSPECT 124
15. MICHAEL JACKSON POSTSCRIPT 127
16. POST- POST-SCRIPT 137
17. MICHAEL JACKSON: THE FINAL WORD 142
18. MICHAEL JACKSON: THOUGHTS ON THE FUNERAL 146
19. A Final Take – Was Michael Jackson a role model for young black males? 150
20. THE LEGACY OF MICHAEL JACKSON 154

"OFF THE WALL SONNETS"
FOR MICHAEL JACKSON

21. PERIODIC BIBLIOGRAPHIC REFERENCE FOR FURTHER RESEARCH 160

22. MICHAEL JACKSON ON TV CREATIVE COMPOSER, 208 SONGWRITER AND HUMAN BEING EXTRAORDINAIRE

"Off the Wall Sonnets" for Michael Jackson Photo. Very early, Michael Jackson earned honorary recognition as a protegee of the Apollon Theater, later to be joined by a whole slew of similarly recognized musical geniuses.

"Off the Wall Sonnets" for Michael Jackson Photo. "The Beginning" of overwhelming sympathy, joy, giving thanks and celebration of the passing of a "great one" who gave so much to so many.

"Off the Wall Sonnets" for Michael Jackson Photo. Notice the "Nat King Cole Walk" street sign juxtaposed to the Apollo Marquee.

"OFF THE WALL SONNETS" FOR MICHAEL JACKSON

"Off the Wall Sonnets" for Michael Jackson Photo. A little "Green Belt" who writes on "Michael's Wall**!"**

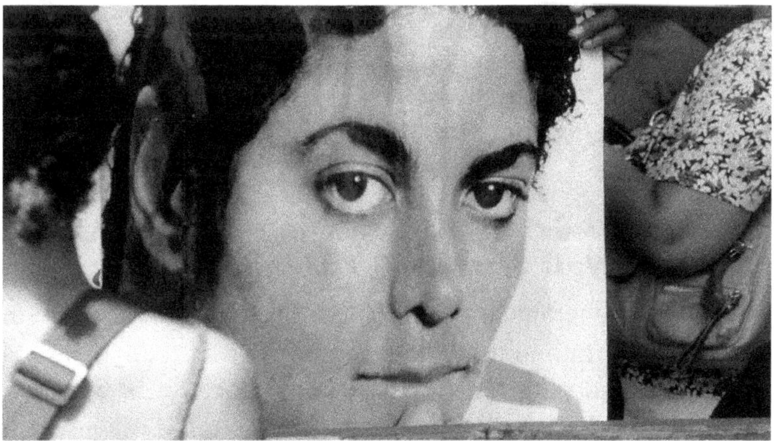

"Off the Wall Sonnets" for Michael Jackson Photo.

"Off the Wall Sonnets" for Michael Jackson Photo. Exuberant image of the great one captured in decorated confetti amidst flowers, candles and teddy bears as lavished by adoring fans whose joyful experiences with Mr. Jackson was shattered in his "Going too Soon!"

"OFF THE WALL SONNETS" FOR MICHAEL JACKSON

"If you want to make the world a better place, take a look at yourself, and make a change." **Michael Jackson**

Introduction I –

THOUGHTS ON MICHAEL JACKSON BY DR. FRED MONDERSON

Michael – The Apollo Memorial, **Revisited** is an attempt to capture photographically the essence and philosophic outpouring of love and affection offered for Michael Jackson, a truly incredible legend and wonderful product of the Apollo Theater where so many have gotten their start. Upon Michael's passing, Rev. Al Sharpton, incisively avant-garde as he always is, called for the celebration not simply to honor this great artiste but also to help shape the overall response that would ensue in wake of Michael's public and private persona. Naturally, because of Michael's great talents that have serenaded so many for so long, the community from far and wide thought it fitting that this magnanimous hero should be remembered Harlem, New York, style. With that in mind, his fans came to give him the thunderous "Wake," "Going Home Party," fitting for the charismatic megastar that Michael really was. In retrospect, with Sharpton stewarding the tribute, the "wolves" were forced to "toe the line" and with that the show beautifully unfolded with thunderous spirituality hovering, musically, mystically and financially rewarding local merchants, as admiring fans swamped the area.

"Off the Wall Sonnets" for Michael Jackson Photo. Evidence of the Memorial Tribute growing upon the "cardboard" reflecting early sentiments of joy and sadness.

To complement the photographs presented in this work, texts praising Mr. Jackson offer different perspectives that constructively chronicle the originality of his life and work as well as countering negative sentiments expressed regarding the gentleman's personal life. This work of praise highlights some aspects of the mystical, spiritual, divine essence of a man who describes himself as "a slave to the rhythm" and as "a perfectionist" who confesses "I am blessed to be an instrument of nature." He had an exceptional work ethic! This is manifest and through his extraordinary talents in which he was able to touch the esoteric metaphysical and spiritual inner core of so many, eschewing a healing potency that speaks to a heavenly mission of human transformation through love, love, love! In addition, as far as possible, paying attention to the significant body of work he has produced and recounting sentiments expressed by the people, this effort has sought to paint as positive a picture of a man whom Elizabeth Taylor dubbed "King of Pop, Rock, Soul, Entertainment." Equally a child star in the public eye just as Michael, she described him as

“OFF THE WALL SONNETS” FOR MICHAEL JACKSON

“highly intelligent, intuitive, understanding, sympathetic and generous” even “larger than life.”

“Off the Wall Sonnets” for Michael Jackson Photo. Two panels of condolence sentiments left by Michael Jackson fans expressing feelings in payback for the joy he gifted the world through his music.

Finally, a bibliography has been appended to encourage further research into the life of this incredible entertainer who knew so many of all walks of life and touched so many more offering sentiments of love, healing and compassion through his magical aura and humanitarian nature. It equally casts a stern and critical view of the role Media has playing in hounding Mr. Jackson with a seeming predetermined intent. While the insidious name calling and negativity is renown, an equally good example is also seen for, in the days after his death word circulated on the Internet that Evan Chandler the young man who accused Mr. Jackson of child molestation, staining his career and persona, has reportedly confessed that "his dad made him falsely swear to those allegations." How sad and even more important, the media has chosen to ignore this revelation unmindful it may make Mr. Jackson rest peacefully knowing the truth will set him free of that horrible experience and to those who have so bitterly excoriated him over the years, make them realize how wrong they were in their harsh treatment to this wonderful soul who only had good intentions in his crusade to help and heal mankind, while gushing them with the joys of music, dance and compassion, amidst tremendous creativity. We should always be mindful of a powerful Michael's saying: "No one wants to be mortal. Everybody wants immortality. I know the creator will die, but his work will live on."

"Off the Wall Sonnets" for Michael Jackson Photo. The "King of Pop" in that great repose!

"OFF THE WALL SONNETS" FOR MICHAEL JACKSON

"The Photographs carry no caption because, for the most part, they can speak for themselves, as they give the reader an opportunity to observe, ponder, reflect and connect to Michael through their own personal experiences they shared with and through him. After all, hardly anyone over the last decades has not heard and participated in the enjoyment of some song associated with Michael Jackson.

"Off the Wall Sonnets" for Michael Jackson Photo. Young "Michael Jackson Impersonator" standing before a crowd of enthusiastic fans!

The Memorial was designed to celebrate a true Apollo legend, someone who went forth and conquered the world through the sensational gracefulness of his dance coupled with the ingenuity of his lyrics and angelic and melodic voice. Putting all of this together, we are convinced there was something special about Michael Jackson, something spiritual, magical even mystical! He was a sort of mythical figure imbued and guided by divine inspiration and heavenly grace. Deepak Chopra described Michael as "one of the great iconic artists of our time." He was an "artistic genius of immense stature and though not formally trained he read classics and listened to Beethoven and Mozart." Even further, Chopra added, Michael Jackson "will be remembered for the agony of what he experienced and the ecstasy he gave people." Equally his son, Gotham Chopra, a friend of Michael for many years added, "The same people who scandalized him turned around to praise him. This is part of the mythical process." That-is-to-say, Michael ascended from mortal to immortal to mythical stature through the profound attributes he possessed.

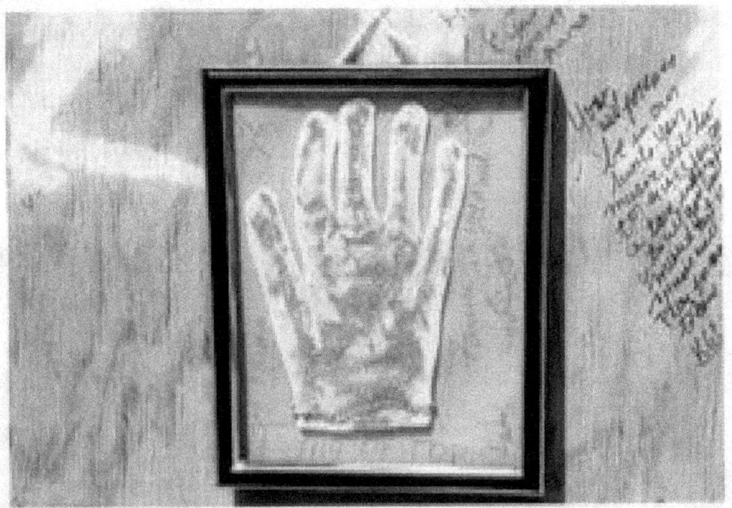

"Off the Wall Sonnets" for Michael Jackson Photo. The famous left-handed glove was a signature part of Mr. Jackson's dress attire.

"OFF THE WALL SONNETS" FOR MICHAEL JACKSON

"Off the Wall Sonnets" for Michael Jackson Photo. An early legend along the path of the Apopllo recognition of musical creativity and cultural greatness.

"Off the Wall Sonnets" for Michael Jackson Photo. "Lights" lit to brighten our Hero's path as a mechanism of his earned heavenly elevation.

"Off the Wall Sonnets" for Michael Jackson Photo. Candles burning bright to light the way to Heaven!

"Off the Wall Sonnets" for Michael Jackson Photo. That Young Michael Jackson Impersonator, again!

"OFF THE WALL SONNETS" FOR MICHAEL JACKSON

"Off the Wall Sonnets" for Michael Jackson Photo. Two gentlemen bringing in the Hero, a significant contribution to the memorial outpouring of love by adoring fans.

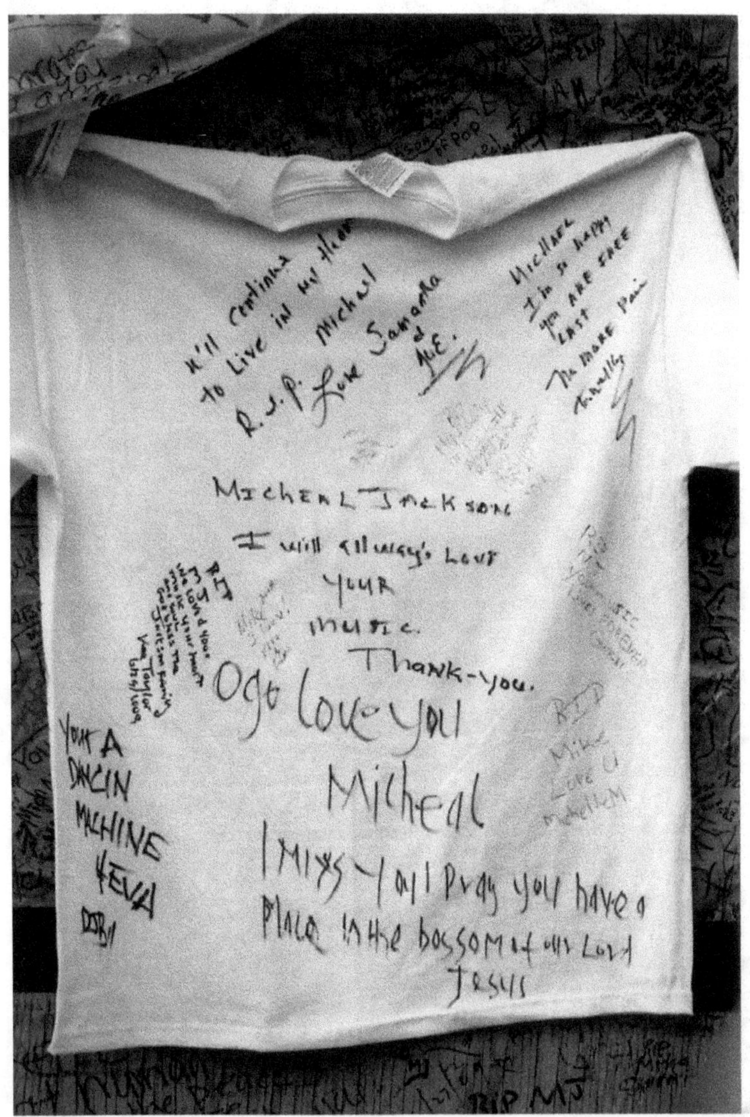

"Off the Wall Sonnets" for Michael Jackson Photo. "T-Shirt culture" on "The Wall" where adoring fans left their "Sonnets."

All of this is sought to be captured in this volume in Tribute to a man of extraordinary artistry who worked tremendously hard to optimize his talents and become the very best in his profession, setting the bar above the rainbow and daring others to even attempt to scale it. Nevertheless, in process of his unspoken challenge, he dared others to do what he did through love, his trust of humanity, all within the philosophical constructs of the "Fatherhood of God and the Brotherhood of Man."

"Off the Wall Sonnets" for Michael Jackson Photo. Fan expressions amidst a T-Shirt photo of young Michael on the wall set up at the Apollo Memorial eliciting tributes to the "Great One!"

"Off the Wall Sonnets" for Michael Jackson Photo. Classic T-Shirt image depicting the creative icon eliciting "Rest in Peace" sentiments.

"OFF THE WALL SONNETS" FOR MICHAEL JACKSON

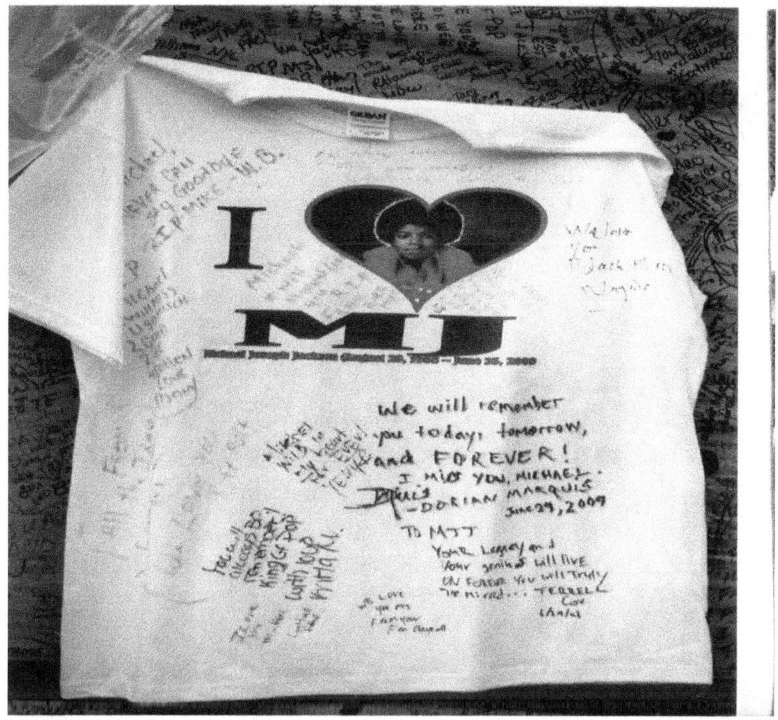

"Off the Wall Sonnets" for Michael Jackson Photo. Michael **FOREVER**!

"Off the Wall Sonnets" for Michael Jackson Photo. Louis Armstrong, pioneer of creative Black, American, creative musical sounds.

"Off the Wall Sonnets" for Michael Jackson Photo. The people have spoken in their "Sonnets!

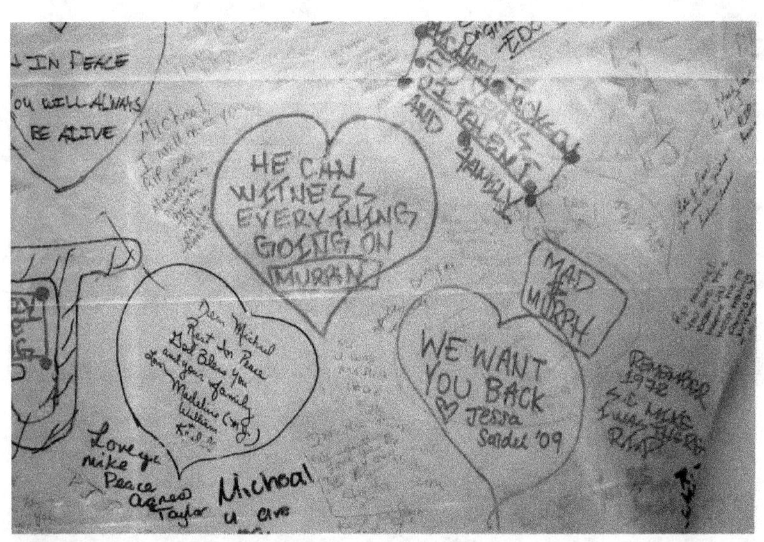

"Off the Wall Sonnets" for Michael Jackson Photo. Sentiments of praise and adoration for the "Great One!"

"OFF THE WALL SONNETS" FOR MICHAEL JACKSON

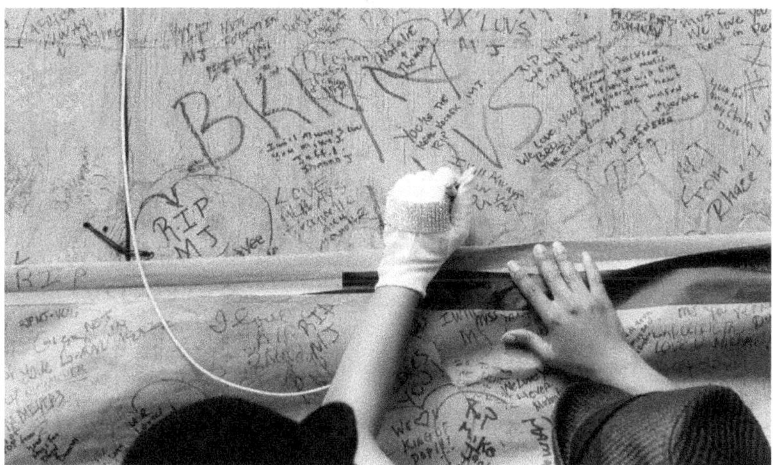

"Off the Wall Sonnets" for Michael Jackson Photo. Reaching high to express sentiments of love for one "Gone too Soon!"

"Let us dream of tomorrow where we can truly love from the soul and know love as the ultimate truth at the heart of all creation." **Michael Jackson**

INTRODUCTION II

THOUGHTS ON MICHAEL JACKSON II BY DR. FRED MONDERSON

Michael Joseph Jackson (5/29/58-6/25/09) was arguably the greatest, if not the greatest entertainer, of all times, certainly the 20th Century. Creatively multi-genius, Michael was an exceptional singer, dancer, songwriter, actor, humanitarian, even coordinator and performer all wrapped in a package of creativity. Just as important, within the dynamics of the many and humungous money or business transactions he was a part of, Michael must have been an exceptional negotiator and businessman. Not to mention, a king living like a king!

All this notwithstanding, as a black man, a successful entertainer and businessman, a sort of "perpetual cash machine," a journalistic and social bullseye became perpetually imprinted on Michael's back. Much of this generated negative publicity. Yet still, the great one continued to create, even dominate the genre of his expertise and therefore the genius became a money-producing spigot that opened him to all manner of potential exploitative scams seeking to extract money from this gentle yet explosive performer, as we know Michael Jackson.

Nonetheless, while such potential negativity lurked in the background with possibilities of stressors on the mental mindset of our hero, the brilliance of his creativity kept producing hit after hit, making money-selling records, singles and albums, building up his fan base, even increasing the acquisition of other entertainers' catalogues of music.

So, at his death, Michael was reported in debt to the extent of some $300-$500 million dollars owed to several creditors; however, Michael's creative greatness matched a not generally known practice of two well-known and successful entertainers, Johnny Cash and Tupac Shakur.

A standard pattern of most entertainers, for example, after a concert performance, there is an "after-party" celebration. With these two gentlemen, on the one hand, instead of celebrating after these functions, they generally return to their studios and continue producing new music, thereby extending their body of work, much to the surprise of people who kept track of production development in the field.

On the Other hand, such a return to the creative factory of the other two musical greats is a trait not to be discounted on the part of Michael Jackson. Notwithstanding, he had an extraordinary skill unknown to many that probably encouraged his peace of mind, his "Bridge over troubled waters." thereby enhancing his generally recognized talent. That is, Michael was a creative painting artist! Let me explain.

After Michael's death in wake of the claims of his indebtedness, Michael's mother, Mrs. Jackson appeared on TV, in a prime-time special with a young man, probably a curator, who revealed the genius' talent. How he was able to paint voluminously pieces and such remained unknown to his watchers! Michael painted and left a warehouse of painting, others not, at the time valued at some $4-billion dollars. Most of his paintings were signed and others were unsigned. So, its imagined, within no time Michael's mother, in charge of his Estate, was able to solve his debt problem! In addition, while there is generally an "after party-party," there is also an "after-death reckoning."

"Off the Wall Sonnets" for Michael Jackson Photo. Journalist and author, Herb Boyd holds a photograph of the Jackson Five in their early years as he, like so many, participated at the Apollo Theater memorial.

When one dies and so not able to create anymore, the value of their body of work generally increases. The quality of the artist's creation determines how they will be remembered by adoring fans, even new generations of music lovers who long for the nostalgic lyrics that captivated contemporaries of the entertainer. That is, while the first or even second year of the artist's death, the rush to secure collector's recordings generally subsides, this has not been the case with Michael Jackson. Year after year, concerns with such matters publish statistics on how much sales were generated by which artist. However, while this writer has not been privy or paid attention to such matters, for the year 2025, it was reported Michael Jackson, among deceased entertainers, had the highest grossing sums of all such records. That year, he made some $160 million dollars from sale of his music, the highest of all such types of sales. As we all know, Michael was no "One Hit Artist," for even today his work seem timeless.

All that notwithstanding, at the time of his death, the TV Commentator on CNN, Donno Brazile reminded, "Michael was big at home, but massive abroad." He, therefore, as a culturally significant "cross-over" entertainer generated an enormous fan-base breaking racial barriers in America, across Western Europe, Asia, Australia, the Caribbean and South America. Thus, in all aspects of human experience, no single individual has had such a giant and universal footprint across the globe appealing to positive loving fans; who, ultimately were saddened by Michael's untimely death.

"OFF THE WALL SONNETS" FOR MICHAEL JACKSON

"Off the Wall Sonnets" for Michael Jackson Photo. Jackie "Moms" Mabley, one of the earliest female comedians and an initial Apollo Theater initial litany of star-power recognition

While much can be said regarding Michael's music, his humanitarian involvement has been significant in advocating, founding and supporting work to assist and help uplift humanity, regardless of race and class. Michael put his money where his heart was, in humanitarian, compassionate causes. Important, in this respect, Michael did not simply throw money at various causes, but he visited the places of such issues and in meeting subjects affected and being served, essentially psychologically and socially cultivated what the American Civil Rights crusader Jesse Jackson emphasized as "Keep Hope Alive."

As such then, Michael Jackson's death, untimely as it was, generated great interest worldwide! So much so, his funeral service at the Staples Center in Los Angeles was estimated to be watched by more than 5 billion people worldwide! Even Prisoners, in their confinement, out of respect, recognizing and feeling the loss of such talent, and more particularly, many may have partied to Michael music, paid him a tribute, thereby emphasizing a "code of prison life conduct."

"Off the Wall Sonnets" for Michael Jackson Photo. Young Impersonator and friend!

Michael's body of musical production reflects unending creativity as he ramped up efforts to remain ahead in the industry keeping in mind he was producing music, doing tours, negotiating and performing concerts, all while negotiating business ventures that included acquiring established musician's music catalogues. All the while challenged by nefarious negative publicity and how to combat wolves battering down his door for the right to publish false reports or to encourage efforts to acquire part of his hard-earned wealth.

“OFF THE WALL SONNETS” FOR MICHAEL JACKSON

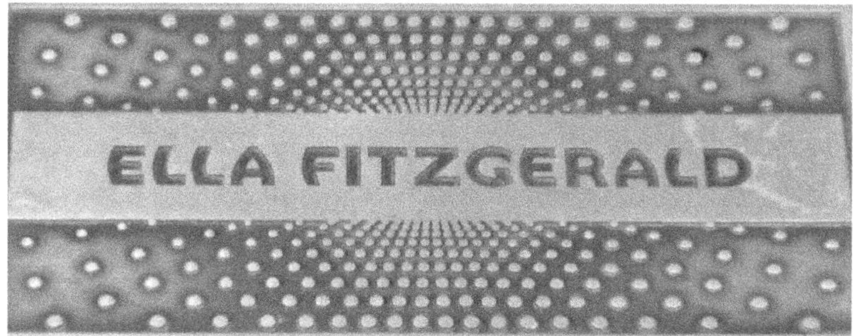

“Off the Wall Sonnets” for Michael Jackson Photo. Ella Fitzgerald. Inspiration to Michael and others.

“Off the Wall Sonnets” for Michael Jackson Photo. Young Michael peering through the wonderful flowery field of thoughtful and heartfelt expressions of sadness and joy for what this iconic gentleman represented as a creative, caring and thoughtful humanitarian.

“In a world filled with hate, we must still dare to hope. In a world filled with anger, we must still dare to comfort. In a world filled with despair, we must still dare to dream. And in a world filled with distrust, we must still dare to believe.” **Michael Jackson**

1. MICHAEL! A Song of Praise By Dr. Fred Monderson

"A wonderful song of praise to a gem of entertainment!"

Beautiful soul, man of love blest with the angelic voice, piece of divinity rests within you
For decades you created an inspiration with a delightful and elegant refinement of sweet musical poetry, seemingly guided by the highest spiritual authority, heart of a gentle lion
Ground-breaking entertainer, the sweet melody of your wonderful craft was superhuman, spiritual, divine, and incandescent, master purveyor of a universal lyrical language
Your inspired music reached across cultures and nations to harmoniously soothe souls of young and old, genius, your innocence is divinely beautiful with a soothing potency

"Off the Wall Sonnets" for Michael Jackson Photo. It is always a Holiday when listening to Billie.

"OFF THE WALL SONNETS" FOR MICHAEL JACKSON

Off the Wall Sonnets to Michael Jackson Photo. The King of Pop in all his exquisite and talented glory!

Adorable and mystical spirit, Michael, archangel, child of exorbitant talent, maker of sweet music of happiness and healing, you are a master commander of musical arenas where your rhythm is classic and explosive, thunderous entertainer extraordinary
Man of boundless vision and magical creativity, how well you play those delectable keys of enchanting music, seeming whatever the poet writes is divinely inspired, professional
Cultural icon, though never echoing black is beautiful with your euphonic voice, existing above mundane issues of blackness

Your life and legacy are manifestations of that forcefully creative shibboleth and the God of Music, Thoth, is pleased with your iconic cultural contribution.

An early view of the entranceway to the Harlem Shrine where well-wishing began to pay tribute to their idol that would later blossom.

Purveyor of happiness through sweet music, imbued with spiritual creativity to create; virtuoso you are a giver of merriment to fans worldwide, your influence is unmatched
Possessing great spiritual grace, merrymaker, your vivid melody charms the soul, engulfs and makes the heart flutter, all wonderfully pleasing to the ear and bosom
Joy maker, your immortal lyrics awaken the dawn, salivates the sun, illuminates the heavens, and soothes evening bloom dressed in gleaming stars of your picturesque attires manifested in colorful garbs, zippers, glasses, white sox, gloves, glitter
Possessing great spiritual vitality, Moonwalker, the best of your superabundant musical charm is pleasing and joyful to the hearing with an original healing potency, unmatched, representing the joy of all humanity

Cultural celebrity phenomenon, your melodic dancing waves and musical expression is poetry in motion, exalting in its chants, everlasting in its blissful exuberance, classical

Great one blest with originality, your spirituality is incredible, your earned immortality is enshrined in photos, images, film, cards, race, music, entertainment, and much more since your talent was before and above your time
Very complicated, yet never racially or culturally controversial, you espoused Godliness in your genius, gentle disposition and soft-spoken mannerism, yet endowed with powerful creative talents you are beyond legend, barrier breaker possessing a loving heart and wonderful disposition, philanthropist who cared for the poor across the globe

"OFF THE WALL SONNETS" FOR MICHAEL JACKSON

"Off the Wall Sonnets" for Michael Jackson Photo. "Michael's fans showing the colors!"

Forcefulness of you as symbol advanced the cause of blackness through culture, music and exquisite harmony that charmed the great mystical beauty and light of the universe
Not just a crossover artiste by any means, your intelligence, stature and persona, global in its consummate perfection, is a testimonial of impressive proportions, soul of genius, existing above our earthly concerns

Brilliant creator of exquisite sounds, you harmoniously impregnated cultural salt in the earth's consciousness, to rejoice and celebrate an enlightening symphony through an amazing body of music, the greatest testament to your extraordinary persona
Extolling love, brotherhood, and cultural syncretism, exalted in your delightful chants
You help others to see,
We are the world, where so many aspire to be

Off the Wall Sonnets to Michael Jackson Photo. Day One of the "Passing" before the excitement through which fans came and paid their revered respect.

Cherubim transcending the realms of the most high, beautiful ornament, wonderful addition to the heavenly choir, your well-mannered, soft-spoken nature is unique
The euphoric melody of your elegant and graceful dancing footsteps partnering with the heavenly and dignified Alvin Ailey

Will forever virtuously echo, Michael, music maker, with the magnificent majesty of Marvin, Miriam, and Marley
As the sweet harmony of your lyrics resonate thunderously in the many mansions of the almighty's silvery universe, an audience of angels will welcome you into divine bosom.

"OFF THE WALL SONNETS" FOR MICHAEL JACKSON

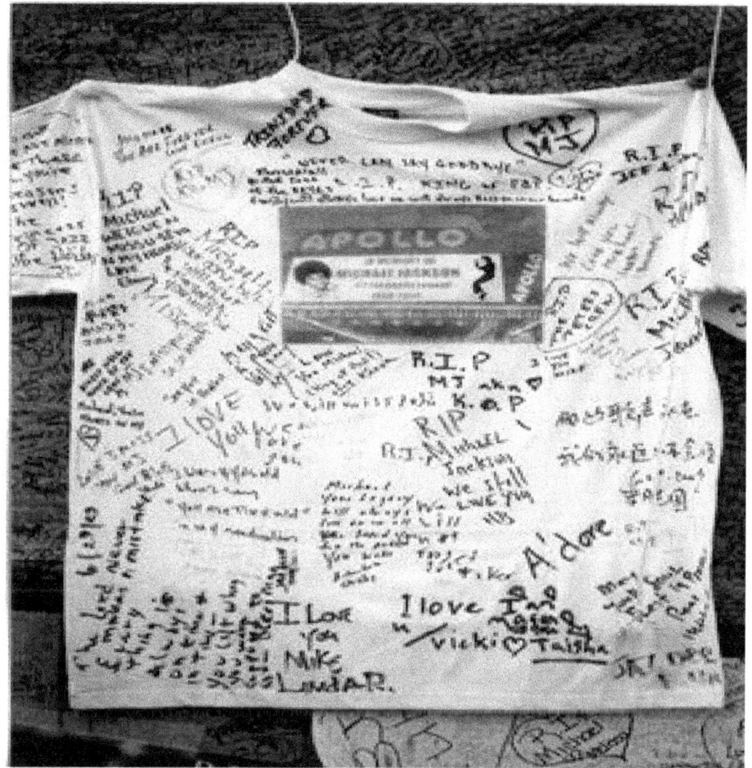

Off the Wall Sonnets to Michael Jackson Photo. The Message is simply "I Love You!"

We mortals continue to sing you praises delightful one, you're more than a crossover star, you were beloved by all
So we can never say goodbye, uniqueness
We will forever be grateful you provided intangible food for the human soul and spirit through your boundless and harmonious musical chords
Trumpeter of splendid chimes, the sweet resonance of your lyrics is like bells chiming musically in the heavenly Milky Way, all resonating into eternity without ending

Hounded in life because of envy, betrayed, yet not guilty, triumphant and martyred for pursuit of creative merriment that pleases the hearts of many cultures, your blessed talent is powerful and everlasting in the celestial firmaments you sang under unending

Off the Wall Sonnets to Michael Jackson Photo. "**Legends Never Die**!"

"Off the Wall Sonnets" for Michael Jackson Photo. The crescendo of joyful thoughts of memories builds for the iconic impresario.

"OFF THE WALL SONNETS" FOR MICHAEL JACKSON

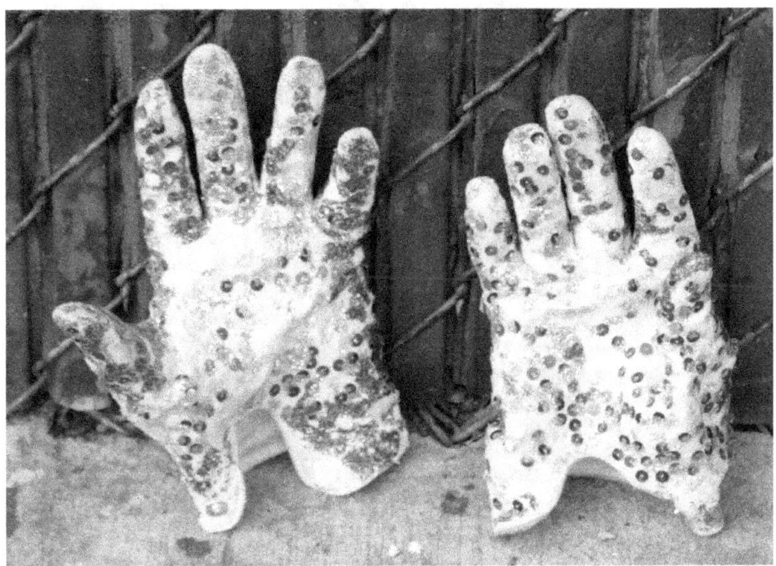

Off the Wall Sonnets to Michael Jackson Photo. This time, two gloves!

"Off the Wall Sonnets" for Michael Jackson Photo. Dionne Warwick will always sing "I Say a Prayer for You," Michael.

Off the Wall Sonnets to Michael Jackson Photo. Harlem came out for Michael!

Today we mourn Knowing your sweet fire will forever burn in your comfortable global domain, soul man King of Pop, talented creator with exceptional artistic charisma, disciplined and a gentle person, man of love in search of love, the deathlessness of your silver sounds and golden harmony will live in musical remembrance for eons to come as the heavens proclaim the mystical and magical genius of your offers to aid humanity

Gifted beyond comparison, beyond legend, yours is music while music lasts, unrivaled, supreme because your mind is a musical instrument of great and melodious refinement, you're considered a universal pop culture icon,

"Off the Wall Sonnets" for Michael Jackson Photo. Sentiments!

Thus, songbird, we give thanks you blest humanity's existence with creative expressions of joyousness, civility and soulful inspiration possessing a tremendously spectacular potency

Your musical and human contributions will echo for generations to come, because your chords reached deep into the universe helping create and echoing the food of divine love

Blessed as an angelic light your magic shined wonderfully bright as a young vigorous sun.

"Off the Wall Sonnets" for Michael Jackson Photo. T-Shirt – "Before and After!"

“OFF THE WALL SONNETS” FOR MICHAEL JACKSON

Bells of heaven chimes as you are called home to embellish the heavenly orchestra

Sorrowfully, we know humanity is deprived when such a soft creative voice of love dies.

“Off the Wall Sonnets” for Michael Jackson Photo. A “Little Green Belt” is among the many Jackson well-wishers standing beneath the Apollo Theater Marquee.

"I love my fans, truly, and deeply. It really makes me happy when I see them content at my shows or when they write me letters and make me drawings. I also love to point my flashlight towards the sky and say, 'I love you' to my beautiful fans." **Michael Jackson**

2. Sonnets, Sentiments of LOVE from the People, His Fans!

1. "Gone but not forgotten. The world is not enough." A. Mays.

2. "**Michael**. An angel has returned to Heaven. **Michael**, God sent you to show us how to love, laugh and live together. My whole life was spent with you in it. I have always and will always love you, My Brother." Michelle Grant, Harlem U.S.A.

3. **Michael and Fawcett** – "You both have a magic that the world never forgets, my hurt turn into good way because, Heaven needs two magically people and God say Welcome. Love You very much. You are not alone! Nana

4. **OUR CHILDMAN BROTHER**. Now they will finally leave you alone!!!

   "We are angry. They never understood your greatness, your style, your class, your spirit. That, artistic beings are a little bit off norm because of their genius. Then there was the legal drug pushers, who we believe sent you away from us much, much too soon! Did greed and envy play a part in all of this? Of course it did! You were caught up in a vicious cycle you couldn't possibly bring yourself out of, our darling brother.

But it's over now, The Father, the Son and the Angels are enjoying that marvelous voice and dance style! Moon Walk for them our brother, make them smile!

Thank you, Our Michael, for being "The ULTIMATE ORIGINAL ENTERTAINER, HUMANITARIAN, GENTLEMAN, and GENTLE MAN!" We will never, ever forget you and there will never be another you! ALL OUR LOVE. Vicki, Vesha, Shannon and Shanni. 6/27/09 Ps. You left us on Shannei's 9th Birthday, so we can never forget you!

5. "**Michael Jackson** will always be remembered in my heart." Love Shantericka Harris.

6. "**God Bless You Michael**. Thank you for bringing us your beautiful music and for being a part of all our lives!" Greg Packer. Huntington, New York.

7. "**Ratcliff Family Loves Mike**." Erie, Pennsylvania.

8. "**MJ** Rules for **LIFE!"**

9. "**RIP MICHAEL JACKSON** – The King of Pop!"

10. "**Michael** – South Africans will never forget when you rocked they shows in 1997. We love Michael Ro Bala Ka Khotic Aubvre Boshoga!" 27/06/09

11. "**Mike** – We will forever feel your love. **RIP**."

12. "**RIP MJ – LOVE YOU. DEE DEE DEANS vs BILLY JEAN**!"

13. "**YOU AND I CHANGE DA WORLD**."

14. We love you **MICHAEL JACKSON R.I.P.**

15. "**SAVE AMERICA – ROCK OPS SHAKE DA CITY**."

16. "We will miss you very much. Your friend." Angel F.

17. "**Safe in God's care**! We love you Michael! Aakira, Brian, Neshie, Ineni, Ellita, Annette, Barbara, Michael, Denise, bob!

18. "We will remember you Today, Tomorrow and Forever!" Dorian Marquis. June 29, 2009

19. "Your legacy and your genius will live on forever. You will truly be missed." Terrell Cox. 6/29/2009

20. "I love you and I am your fan."

21. "You will always be remembered, **King of Pop**!"

22. "I love you, my angel."

23. "**Michael Jackson** One Love."

24. "**RIP MJ** – I love you. 'Your Wife!'" Denise Meterer.

15. "We love you, **Michael**!" Jamel.

16. "**R.I.P. M.J**. We Love You. Love" – Sitcom Kciber

"OFF THE WALL SONNETS" FOR MICHAEL JACKSON

17. "**Michael**. You touched all in our hearts and made us so proud. U are the Original Dancing Machine! LOVE!" – The Greene Family

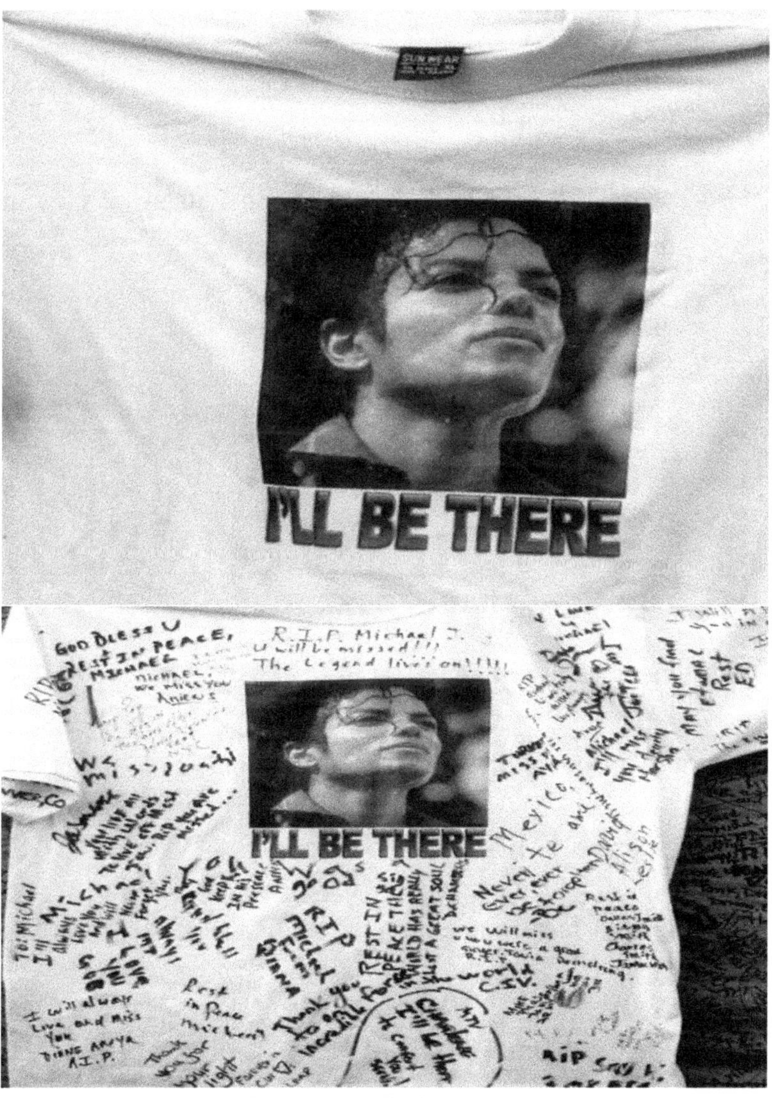

"Off the Wall Sonnets" for Michael Jackson Photo. "Before and After" expressing loving sentiments.

18. "**LOVE YOU MICHAEL**! Thanks for y our Love, and you will forever live in my heart. R.I.P." Tracey Ruff

19. "I Love You **Mike**." Love. Dominique 6/29/09

20. "**MICHAEL**. You the Fucking Best. Fuck Press. Love." Toya J.

21. "**MICHAEL JACKSON**. You will always be in my heart! Love You!" Crystal T (**PYT**)

22. "**MIKE**. I Luv U. R.I.O" Akinwin.

23. "Mary Lewis prays for U!" 6/29.09 **R.I.P**.

24. "You Leave us too soon. I need you. Keep dancing and singing, Please!"

25. "**R.I.P. Michael Jackson** 1958-2009."

26. "**R.I.P**. **MICHAEL**. **King of Pop**.

27. "We Love you, **Michael**. Dow, Jamal, Sertie

28. "We Will Miss You. You changed the world! **R.I.P.** And I will always remember you. Your music will always mean something to me. **I LOVE** you forever!"

29. "**MICHAEL. WE LOVE YOU. R.I.P**." The Rabanal Family

30. "We Love You **Michael**." Denise Dossyl

"OFF THE WALL SONNETS" FOR MICHAEL JACKSON

31. "You will always be loved and remembered. We will miss U!" D. Mint.

32. "**R.I.P**. You were the Best!" G.B.

33. "**MJ**. You rocked my world!"

34. "Remember the first time!"

35. "**Michael**, we will always love you!"

36. "There will never be another **King of Pop**!"

37. "You are the best!" G.B.

38. "**Michael**, you changed the world of Music. We loved you." Michelle J. Shalla.

39. "You are My Soul Mate!"

40. "You rocked my world. You know you did"

41. "**R.I.P. LOVE ALWAYS**!"

42. "The Greatest. Love You, **Mike**."

42. "God Bless You, **Michael**. Thank you for bringing us your beautiful music and for being a part of all our lives!!" Greg Packer, Huntington, N.Y.

43. "You were the Best." G.B.

44. "**Michael**. Love will always win the day."

45. "You rocked

my world. You know you did.?"

46. "**Michael**, you changed the world. We Loved you." Michelle J.

47. "The Darkest Cloud. Let the sky cry for Mike." **M.J**.

48. "We love you babe. Go to higher heights in heaven."

49. "May Allah Guide and Protect your Soul"

50. "**R.I.P**. You Loved, Jones."

51. "**Michael**, No one will ever forget You. I love you."

52. "The greatest of all time!!!" "Your Wife" Alon and Ori.

53. "**Michael**, you will always be the **King of Pop**. You will be missed."

54. "Will Love you Forever." Melanie

55. "**Mike**, you were the best that ever did it!"

56. "God bless the **King of Pop**." Byron

57. "**Michael. RIP**. God knows best. Thank you for the joy you put in my home. You will be missed." Gina Johnson, Far Rockaway

58. "Don't stop till you get enough, **Mike**." **PYT**

59. "There will never be another." **R.I.P. M.J**. – Ermese

60. "We will miss you. Love." Janiva

"OFF THE WALL SONNETS" FOR MICHAEL JACKSON

61. "Rest now, **Michael**. Love" Melanie

62. "**Michael**, you were one of kind, and there will never be another you. May you find peace in death. You were my love."

63. **Mike**. I know you are much happier in heaven rather than being in this hell on earth." Tiffany

64. "**R.I.P. MJ**." SB

65. "Ainsley Harris" (Kegs)

66. "**Michael, Rest in Peace**. You are loved"

67. "**R.I.P. Michael**." Doria

68. "Love Yah, **Michael**. R.I.P." Daphnae Hicks.

69. "We will always love you!" Sol

70. "We will always remember you!" East Side, West Side Spanish friends

71. Jameo, N.Y. "Love Always!"

72. "God Bless You **Michael**. From Kim Johnson

73. "A true Icon. U will be remembered 4-ever and my kids will grow up listening to you. **R.I.P**. **King of Pop**." Love Conover

74. "Thanks for sharing your love of music. You will be missed."

75. "Words can't describe how much you mean to me. You are my idol. **R.I.P**." Dyann P.

76. "**Please be at Rest**. Let the pain subside." Nicole

77. "Fare Well!" Thomas and Senay

78. "Miss you Much!"

79. "We can't believe you are gone. You will always be missed." Susan

80. "We'll sure miss you, **Michael**" Marolene

81. "Dare you rest in peace. **Mike**." N. Diop

82. "Tonya Loves you, **Mike**."

83. "You were my first love!"

84. "Thank you for all the good times."

85. "I have been a fan since a child. I will miss you always. Love you."

86. "6/27/09 – "**Michael** you are loved!" Carrie J.

87. "Long Live a King. King of all Music. I will truly miss 4-ever!" K.

88. "We will always Love You!" Nehanda.

89. "Love! Your biggest Fan!"

90. "Greatest of All Time."

"OFF THE WALL SONNETS" FOR MICHAEL JACKSON

91. "**R.I.P. Michael**!" Danell

92. "**R.I.P. MJ**."

93. "You will never, ever, be forgotten. When that grove, sad and gone, you find that love survives, so that we can rock 4-ever on…"

94. "Rock with you!"

95. "**Rest in Peace Michael**. Love!" Kimoni Stephens

96. "I will always love you!" Karen

97. "Love you always!"

98. "**Michael**. Rockaway Loves Ya." L. Louise

99. "Gone but never forgotten." Faragott

"Off the Wall Sonnets" for Michael Jackson Photo. Clearly an image before ascension to divine stardom status.

100. "**R.I.P. M.J**. Big fan." Jo. Bro.

101. "Ainsley Harris (Kegs)."

102. "**Michael**! **Rest in Peace**. You are loved!" Diana

103. "We will always Love U." Nehanda

104. "I will truly miss you 4-ever." K

105. "**R.I.P**. **Michael**. Love." Latrellya M.

106. "There are those who can be duplicated. That word will never be applied towards you. RIP." C.L.E.

107. "Love Ol You." Michael Trinap

108. "God Bless you and your family!"

109. "Love you, **Michael**." Lynda

110. "You the best thing that ever happened to Music! See you later." H. Javereweo.

111. "There was none greater." A. Badx

112. "**Michael**, you mean so much to me! As a child living in Burton, La Covia, St. Elizabeth, Jamaica, I listened to your songs. I wrote my own lyrics to 'The Girl is Mine.' I am in shock! I wanted this to come back for you." Junior, Tina, Shanique, and Johnoie!

"OFF THE WALL SONNETS" FOR MICHAEL JACKSON

113. "What can I say, you are the best and I write this on behalf of 'I can't stop crying. A great humanitarian Love.'"

114. "**R.I.P. Michael**. Forever!"

115. "You will forever be in our heart."

116. "**Michael, Rest in Peace**. I love your music." Jenna

117. "You will forever be in our hearts. Your music will live forever. You are a love inspiration to all. You were well-meaning and your music will play for years to come." K.E.C.

118. "Forever in my mind. Love." Koneis C.

119. "There will never be another! **R.I.P. M.J**." Ermese

120. "**R.I.P. POP KING**."

121. "**RIP. M.J**." S.B.

122. "Thank you for the music."

123. "Thank you. Love!" Bella and Kevin

124. "God Bless. **King of Pop.**" Byron

125. "**Mike**. You were the best that ever did it." Cleon

126. "Love You. Angel Jackson"

127. "I know you are much happier in Heaven than in Hell on Earth.

128. "I Love You." Tiffany

129. "Thank you for the Music and the Love. **R.I.P**. **Michael**."

130. "Gigi Joseph"

130. "Words cannot describe how much you mean to all. You're my idol. **R.I.P**." Damn!

131. "Africa Love You."

132. "Love." Yvonne

133. "You're the best." Dalbert and Nancy

134. "You will always be the **King of Pop** forever. You will be blessed. Love." Renee Watts. August 2009

135. "**Michael Jackson**. The Greatest Legend for all time. May you rest in peace." Tricia

136. "May God keep your spirit in Peace." B.W. 1958

137. **R.I.P**. You're in a Better Place. Love U. Stella!!!"

138. "AMELIA!"

139. "We Love you and miss you. Forever in our hearts." Ly and Family

140. Ciara Wiley. NC 2009. "**R.I.P**. **Michael** We Love you!"

141. "**R.I.P**. **Michael Jackson**. You Rock." Alex B.

"OFF THE WALL SONNETS" FOR MICHAEL JACKSON

142. "**Rest in Peace Michael**." From Stella. "We Love you. Till we meet again"

143. "We luv U, babe – Go to higher heights in heaven."

144. "**R.I.P. Mike**. Love" Deb

145. "JAH Bless You."

146. "Remember the first time." Dawn and Dunn Family

147. "Let the sky cry for more."

148. "You were loved." D. Jones.

149. "**R.I.P. Michael**. you're the Greatest!" Br. Julio B.

150. "**Michael**. **Rest in Peace**. I love your music." Jema

154. "Thank you." Bella and Kevin

155. "**Rest in Peace**, **Michael**"

156. "Rest now, **Michael**" Melanie

157. "**Rest in Peace Michael**. Love." Lorna F.

158. 7/27/09 – Bobbie Walker "Miss you **Michael Jackson**."

159. "Thank you, God for your gifts to us. We love you, **Michael**." Azater.

160. "**Rest in Peace**." Beverley

161. "**King of Pop**!"

162. "**Michael**, we love you."

163, "**LOVE**, **LOVE**, **LOVE**!" **Daisy** 2009 – "Love Ya!"

164. "Live, Love, People!"

165. "**R.I.P**. You will be greatly missed and forever in our Love!" Vineshia

166. "**R.I.P**. The True King!"

167. "I Love U **Michael**." Restin D.

168. "Live Love People."

169. "**R.I.P**. **Michael**!" Michele

170. "Love **Michael**." Kim King

171. "**M.J. FOREVER**!"

172. "**R.I.P**. **M.J**." K.

173. "**Rest in Peace**. Tina Bilambo

174. "**R.I.P. Michael**. We will miss you!" Jameclak AKA Jay Mills

175. "We'll Miss You!" Jon Taylor

176. "**Rest in Peace**!" Tina Bilambo

“OFF THE WALL SONNETS” FOR MICHAEL JACKSON

177. DJ Raye Bender – Music Blender – “**Michael Jackson for Ever**!”

178. “The way you make me feel … SAD – LOVE. See you in Heaven!”

179. “To **Michael Jackson**. We Love you!” From Nysjah, Pat, Joy, Kearna, Kyle, and Ricky

180. “**MJ RULES FOR LIFE**! Always and forever. We love You.”

181. “We The People – 6/25.2009”

182. “**MJ**. **R.I.P**.” Liz P.

183. “**RIP**. **Michael Jackson** – We Still Love You.” H.I.J.

184. “Trinidad Forever. LOVE”

185. “LOVE. I miss you, God Bless.”

186. “The Lord Never makes mistakes. Everything is always on time and in time.”

187. “I Love U!” Vicki

188. “**Michael Jackson** - We still love you!” H.B

189. A’DORE. “**R.I.P**. **M.J**.”

190. “I Love you. We Love You”

191. “We Will Miss You!”

192. “You are the world!”

193. “We will always love You, **Michael J**.”

194. “**R.I.P**. **Michael J**.”

195. “I am madly in love with **Michael**!”

196. “May your soul rest in peace!”

197. “Love. I miss you **M.J**. God Bless You!”

198. “May you **Rest in Peace**!”

199. “**R.I.P**. **MJ**” – aka K.A.P

200. “Jesus loves pop! You never die.” Manuela (Costa Rica)

201. “God Bless”! Anneye 6/27/09

202. “**R.I.P**. **Michael**!’

203. “You showed me to follow my dreams and don’t stop till I get enough.” Yenira DeJour 2009

204. “My world will never be the same. Damn, I make sure you are never forgotten.” X-Charles

205. “**R.I.P**. **MJ**.” Kelli

206. “**MJ**. **Harlem** Loves You! I Love You” Haile King Rubie. Harlem Artist.

207. “I Love You.”

"OFF THE WALL SONNETS" FOR MICHAEL JACKSON

208. "Gone too soon!"

209. "I will miss you, or We will miss you. We will always love you." P. Kelny

210. "**Michael**. Never can say goodbye! **R.I.P**. **MIKE**." W.B.

211. "We love you, **Black Man**." Nayaba

212. "**Michael**. We will miss you so much! Too good to be forgotten. LOVE." Ebony

213. "We will remember you today, tomorrow and **FOREVER**. I miss you, Michael." Dupius-Dorian Marquis June 29, 2009

214. "**Michael** Will be in my heart forever." Yeny R.

215. "We will **miss you** very much. Your friend!" Angela

216. "Safe in God's care! We love you, Michael!" Akila, Brian, Nestia, Ineni, Ellita, Annette, Barbara, Michael, Denise, Bob!

217. "**Michael**, your music lives!" Malik

218. "The **Greatest**. Love you, Mike."

219. "**R.I.P**. Love you **Michael**." Michelle M.

220. "Ago Love You, **Michael**. I miss you. I pray you have a place in the bosom of Our Lord Jesus!"

221. "**Michael Jackson**. I will always love your music. Thank you."

222. "**R.I.P**. **M.J**. Your music lives **forever**." Oneal

223. "Mike, I love you now and **forever**."

224. "You'll continue to live in my heart, **Michael**. **R.I.P**."

225. "**Michael**, I'm so happy you are free at last. No more pain!" Trually

226. "**R.I.P. M.J**. We loved your music, your heart and soul. **Jackson Family**." Vera Taylon – 6/29/2009

227. "**R.I.P**. My family and I will remember you!" Panyinder – 0/9

228. "**Mike**, I love U." Vera

229. "**Michael**, you got me through the tough times!"

230. "Jamaicans say LOVE!"

231. "**R.I.P**. Dam Man!"

232. "**Mike**, we love" Charles Clay

233. "Antoine the King. **Michael** the Man. **Forever**!"

234. "**R.I.P**" Brownsville! 2009

235. From Junior. "**MJ**. We will truly miss your music, your kindness and love for Xmas. You inspired the

world in ways that nobody understood. Your music brought joy, entertainment for humanity and happiness to everyone. Your music made me Feel happy in every way. May you **R.I.P**. I LOVE U!

236. From Kenneth. "We will miss you. You changed the world! **R.I.P**. and I will always remember. Your music will always mean something to me. I LOVE you forever!"

237. "I love you. Much Love. Dominique – 6/29/09

238. **Michael**. Thanks. Your love and you will **forever** live in my heart. **R.I.P**." Tracey Ruff

239. "**Michael**. You have blessed so many with your presence and your music. You have and will always be an Icon. Love always!" Myisha, Kelvin and Kelvin Michael J.R.

240. "**Michael**. I am happy you are free forever!" Junior

241. "**Michael**, you touched all our hearts and we are so proud. You are the original dancing machine. Love!" The Greene Family

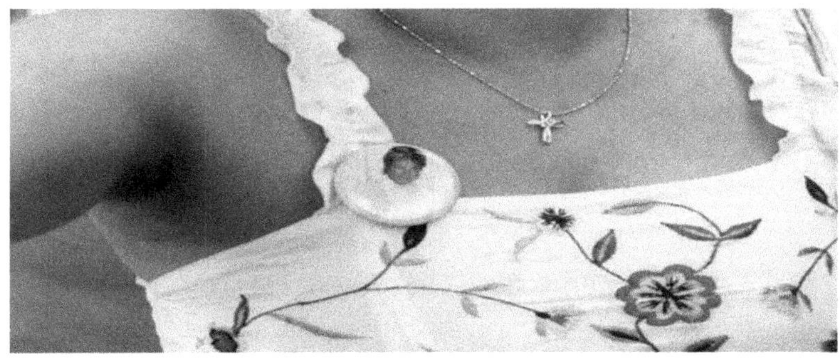

"Off the Wall Sonnets" for Michael Jackson Photo. A button expressing love on the right side of the heart.

"Off the Wall Sonnets" for Michael Jackson Photo. There's that "Little Green Belt" signing "The Great Wall!"

242. "Save America. Roc Ops. Shake Da City."

244. "The Greatest! Love you, Mike."

"OFF THE WALL SONNETS" FOR MICHAEL JACKSON

245. "You'll always be Love."

246. "Love You **MJ**."

247. "We will miss you. Love!" Tanira

248. "Don't stop till you get enough!"

249. "There will never be another. **R.I.P**. **M.J**." Ermese

250. "Love you, **Michael**!" H.E.

251, "You are not alone, forever now!"

252. "**Rest in Peace**, MJ"

253. "Love you Man, Rasta!"

254. "I will miss you. **Rest in Peace**." Tina Bilari Bo

255. "**Michael**, Miss you Forever." Be Joy

256. "DJ Ray Pender, The Music Blender. Thank you **Michael Jackson**, the Best Ever!"

257. "Miss You, dancing Machine." Ronne Hayme

258. "**RIP MJ**." K.B.

259. "The way you make me feel … Sad. See You in Music Heaven!"

260. "**RIP MJ** – **KING OF POP** – A Genius!"

261. "God Bless." Myrna

262. "You can dance. Love! Jaymie!

263. "With Love, **Mike**. Always!" S.D

264. "**RIP Michael**. God Bless!"

265. "**Michael**. I Love You." Gina

266. "Love you **Michael**" Angel

"Off the Wall Sonnets" for Michael Jackson Photo. "Flying high in the friendly sky!"

267. "I Know Your Still Flying!"

268. "**RIP** Majic Jack! ILYSM." Coco and Sheeba

269. "God needed to learn how to Moonwalk! I Love U!" M.J.

270. "We Love You and Wish You Peace!"

"OFF THE WALL SONNETS" FOR MICHAEL JACKSON

271. "Chico. 3W Loves M.J."

272. "We still will hear Ya!"

273. "I will miss U and I, or we will always Love U!" Kelvin C.

274. "I will always Love You!"

275. "Gone Too Soon!"

276. **MJ**, We Love You!" Wendy

277. "Gigi!"

278. "**Michael**, We Will Meet Again! Love" M.E.

279. "**R.I.P**! Love!" Kathy

280. "We Love You, **Michael**. God Bless!" B. Kids

281. "A little part of me went with you! I Love you!"

282. "**R.I.P. MJ**!" HOFFA 140

283. "Thank You **Michael** 4 moving my wonder years!" Bea Panda

284. "I Love You. You did Beat It; You Beat the Odds!" Arlene

285. "**R.I.P**. **MJ**. I'm Gonna Miss U! Love!" Daggamal Dirty Feddi

286. "Mary Lewis Prays for M. 6/29/2009 R.I.P."

287. "3Diox.Bal.com" MJD

288. "Romil and Rose!"

289. "**Mike**. I Lov U. Akiwon. **R.I.P**"

290. "We Luv You. Judy and Cleo. **R.I.P**. "

291. "I Miss You." Latrell

292. "**MJ**. You're Music will be a part of Us 4-Ever." Joanna

293. "I will miss you!" Nettie

294. "You are the best!"

295. "Love You **Mike**!" Love Lord Superb of Far Rock, America

296. "**R.I.P Michael**. You will Always be Alive." Caaleb

297. "6/29/09 – God Bless **Michael**. Enjoy many moments with the Angels." Linda Mills

298. "We love you, **Michael**. I really hope you Rest in Peace." Deborah A. Davis.

299. "You are the Best!"

300. "Gigi. I love you **Michael**, the King of Pop! You are my Idol!"

301. "You are not Alone!"

"OFF THE WALL SONNETS" FOR MICHAEL JACKSON

302. "Your Songs **Forever**!" Norman Gollan

303. "Alexis. **R.I.P**. We Love U. Miss you a lot. **King of Pop**! You're in a better place."

304. "Memories. We Love You." Pia K.

305. "From Liz. I Love You **Michael**. You have always brought me joy with your music, the wonderful things you did for the world. You were 1 of a kind and a gentle kind soul that we were blest to have with us. No one can compare to you. R.I.P. I LOVE U!"

306. "I Love **MJ**." Mildred

307. "**R.I.P**. **MJ**!" Bret Paul

308. "Love Always." Penny

309. "**MJ** GOAT!"

310. "**R.I.P**. **MJ**"

311. "Love You. **MJ**." Freddy

312. "Stay Black!"

313. "Love Essence!"

314. "**Michael J**. Maintains to be the Greatest of All Time." Murphy

315. "Love You." Vicky Joseph

316. "Always in My Heart!" Bettie McIntyre

317. "Love **Forever**. Your biggest Fan." Jen

318. "**R.I.P**. Love You Save."

319. "Fanness!"

320. "Can't Stop Crying! You are truly missed." Deidre and Tony

321. "Love You **MJ**!" Freddy

322. "Our hearts go out to the **Jackson Family** and we will keep Michael in our prayers. He has been a great inspiration to me throughout my lifetime. His music is unchallenged and unique and nothing or no other great entertainers in this world will ever replace him or his music." Love You. **MJ**"

324. "Love Always." Benita

325. "Karen Mobley and Family LOVE YOU. True Motown Detroiters!"

326. "You are now our Angel of Music!

327. "**R.I.P**." Lenny Patterson

328. "**R.I.P**. Love You. Rab225" B.P.

329. "We love MJ with all our hearts **KING OF POP**!"

330. "DJ Lovely – **R.I.P. MIKE**"

331. "YOU ARE THE LIGHT OF THE WORLD!

332. "You are free. Love You MJ."

"OFF THE WALL SONNETS" FOR MICHAEL JACKSON

333. "Eugene Loves **Michael**."

335. "Boogie Down Bronx!"

336. "We Love **Michael J**." J. Jeff. To the Left!"

337. "**King of Pop** 4-Ever. Love. **R.I.P**."

338. "Love You Michael. Miss You

339. "Love You **Michael J**. God Bless You and the Jacksons!"

340. "**R.I.P**. Love Always." Tyren

341. "Keith. **R.I.P**. **MJ**!"

342. "We love you. MJ. LOVE!" Aviana Collado

343. "**R.I.P**. M.J. 4-Ever." 181

344. "Love You. **R.I.P**." Dominique

345. "Love You **Forever**, **Michael**." Allison and Kadisha

346. "**R.I.P**. **Michael Jackson**." Delicia Love.

347. "Rest in Peace. Love **Forever**." Munchie

348. "Call MY Name, I'll Be There!" Lorraine Gaskin

349. "**Michael**, You Will Always be Loved and Missed!"

Anni Sweeney and Donegial Ireland

350. "**R.I.P. Michael**!" Slafice

351. "WE LOVE YOU **MICHAEL**. Deborah Ann Davis 97th Street- 6/29/09

352. "You are always in our hearts." Michelle Steinmann

353. "**MJ**, Fendi P. Loves You Mucho. U Will Always be T7-Remembered."

354. "Romania. We Love You **MJ**!" Cristina Ross

355. "**R.I.P. MICHAEL** – **HARLEM** LOVES YOU!"

356. "**M.J**. LOVE"

357. "God Picked a Flower!"

358. "**R.I.P**."

359. "**R.I.P. Michael**." Slobhan "Sibby" Simpson 6/28/09

360. "LOVE!" Joseph Wiley

361. "I Love You **Michael**, R.I.P." DRS

362. "**Rest in Peace**. You Will always Be Alive"

363. "MAD MONEY MURPH!"

364. "**MICHAEL JACKSON**. 50 years of talent and family!"

"OFF THE WALL SONNETS" FOR MICHAEL JACKSON

365. "We Want You Back!"

366. "Love You Mike. **Peace**." Agnes Taylor

367. "**Michael**, you are very talented."

368. Dear **Michael**. **Rest in Peace**. God Bless You and Your Family. Love." Madeline William (NJ)

369. "**Michael**, I will miss you. **R.I.P**. LOVE" Nadine, Dominique.

370. "**Mike**" God Bless You."

371. Ross J. "**Michael Jackson**, I Love you, Yes!"

372. "THRILLER" Nageel Thompson, "**R.I.P**. **MJ**."

373. "MISSION COMPLETE, **MJ**!"

374. "To the King Himself. You are loved by millions!"

375. "LOVE" Syraj Herbert

376. "We Will Miss You!"

377. "**R.I.P**. **KING OF POP MJ**."

378. "Love You. Boobie Beatrice" DOLL Johnson, Patterson, NJ 6/28.09

379. "I Love You **Michael** 4-Ever." Davide

380. J. Hinjos. "X-Tra Love from the J Hinjos - "Man in the Mirror!"

381. "**R.I.P**. **Michael**. Even though I was scared of you when I was Younger, you will be miss." L.W. Teka

382. "Some may hate you. You will always be in my Heart."

383. "Love you, **Michael**. **Rest in Peace**" Corine

384. "You Will Be Missed. MY God Bless You in **Heaven**. Love You. From Michael Green

385. "**R.I.P**. LOVE YOU ALWAYS. Love" Vanity

386. "Love U, We Will Miss You

387. "**R.I.P**. **MJ**. LUV YA!"

388. "**REST IN PEACE**."

389. "You are the Greatest of All Time and your music will live on for all Eternity. Love! Heather from NJ

390. "You are the Best **Michael**." Michelle and Kids

391. "You're the Greatest!"

392. "**R.I.P**. **MICHAEL**. Love you Always." Christiana

393. "MUCH LUV!"

394. **MICHAEL JACKSON** (1958-2009) – May God Bless the Jackson Family Always! Michael you will be in My Heart Always. May you **Rest in Peace** and May God Bless You and Forgive you for the things they said you did. We are all sinners in one way or

another, No one is perfect. You were bad in your music and dancing. WHO BAD!" Donna Jean

395. "**Rest in Peace Michael**! And thank you for all the years of Entertainment. I love you and you will be missed. God Bless You! Kathy Z. 6/27/09

396. "**God Bless You**. **Michael**. Your music, your dancing, your extraordinary talent. Will be remembered for ever. I Love you so much. We will be missing you. LOVE" Simon A.

397. "Like Your Sons. 'Gone Too Soon'" Kathy

398. "I used to be scared of you but Now I love you.

399. "You left way too soon. You change music forever!"

400. "We Love You **Mike**!" M. Jackson

401. "Love **Michael Forever**! The Thomas Family

402. "Angel of Beloved Messenger, you tore all stereotypes and showed us the way to save the world and ourselves is through **LOVE**, **UNITY**, **PEACE**' **ACCEPTANCE BUT ABOVE ALL LOVE**. Thank you for your true love and gifts you gave to us all forever. R.I.P. I love you and will miss you. Thank you." A. Rodriguez

403. Nyasia. **I Love you**. Love the song 'Beat it'"

404. "**Michael**. You Will be Missed." Lisa

405. "**R.I.P**. **MJ**." Tyese Wilson

406. "**R.I.P**. **King of Pop**. Love." The Shelby's

407. "**R.I.P**. **MJ**. You're gone but never forgotten." Terry

408. "To the Gloved One. You will be missed."

409. "**MIKE**. **R.I.P**. I LOVE ALWAYS." Granell

410. "Viaje Gracias"

411. "**Mike**. Rest in Peace. You will be forever Missed. Thriller!"

412, "**R.I.P**. **Michael**. Lilly and I will miss your Majesty."

413. "**R.I.P**. You were and always was right with me.

414. "I Love you, **Michael**. Rest in peace, really. Thank you for everything." Amy

415. "I Love you Michael." Restin D.

416. "**MJ** Forever!"

417. "**R.I.P**. **Michael**." From Diana

418. 'Mexico Te Amo." David Alison Leslie

419. "May you find Eternal Rest!" Ed

420. "**Michael**. I'll miss you dearly" Marsha

421. "God Bless You. "**R.I.P**. **Michael**. U will be missed!!! - The Legend lives on!!!!! Peace Michael."

"OFF THE WALL SONNETS" FOR MICHAEL JACKSON

422. "You're a dancing Machine." Keeva

423. "I Miss you. I pray you have a place in the bosom of Our Lord **Jesus**."

424. "You will be greatly missed and forever in our hearts." Vineshia

425. "**R.I.P**." Tia

426. "**R.I.P**. The Icon!"

427. "**R.I.P**." D'Nasia

428. "God made you Special!"

/429. "There will never be another!"

430. "You will always be the Best!"

431. "May your Soul Rest!"

432. "**R.I.P** Love You. Smooth Criminal."

433. "**R.I.P**. The Man, The Legend!"

434. "Your greatest hit moved us. We miss you **Michael**!"

435. "**Michael Jackson**. Amazing. More than Amazing!"

436. "**R.I.P**. **Mike**. Love!" Izzy – Detroit!!

437. "**R.I.P**. **MJ**!"

438. "True and Great Inspiration. Love You **Forever**!"

439. "Always and 4-Eva. WE LOVE YOU. WE THE PEOPLE, 6/25/2009

440. "Gabby LOVE Y ou!"

441. "**R.I.P**. **MJ** God Bless You." Gina

442. "Missing You. Dancing Machine!" Ronne Hayme

443. "The way you make me feel. … sad. LOVE. See you in musician Heaven. Kim Harris

444. "Praise the Lord!"

445. "We will miss you!" Jon Taylor

446. "Love You **Michael**!"

447. "To **Michael Jackson**! We Love You." From Nysjha, Pat, Joy, Kinera, and Tricky

448. "With Love Always!"

449. "**R.I.P**. **MIKE**. We will miss you!" Jameekah AKA Jay Mills

450. "You can Dance. Love!" Jamie

451. "**MJ**. Love You!"

452. "Merci per les emotions. Love." Nathalie

453. "I Love You!" Joy

"OFF THE WALL SONNETS" FOR MICHAEL JACKSON

454. "**MIKE** 4 LIFE!"

455. "Love You, **MJ**!"

456. "Rest in Peace!" K. Daddy Piedo

457. "May your soul rest in peace!" Joy Wigley 6/26

458. "**R.I.P**. Love You. Smooth Criminal!"

459. "We Will Miss You!"

460. "Thank You, **Michael**!"

461. "Your greatest hit moved us. We love you, **Michael**."

462. "**MJ** - **R.I.P**." Liz P.

463. "You will always be with us in memory." Kerry

464. "LIVE, LOVE, PEOPLE!"

465. "**R.I.P**. THE TRUE KING!"

466. "I Love You **Michael**!! Roslin D.

467. "**R.I.P**!" D'Nasia

468. "There are those who can be duplicated. That word can never be implied towards you. **R.I.P**."

469. "Love you **Michael**!" Lindo

470. "Love You, **Michael**!" Trinap

471. "God Bless You and Your Family."

472. "I know You are in Heaven!" D.T.

473. "There was none Greater!"

474. "**MJ**. You are the only **King of Pop**!"

475. "**Michael**, Rockaway Loves Ya!" R.I.P!"

476. "LOVE!" Donna Tulloch

477. "**R.I.P**. FOREVER **Michael**." Lorna Pagan

478. "Thank you God for your gift to us. How you moved!"

479. "Gone but never forgotten!"

480. "I will always Love You!" Karen

481. "**Michael**. You are the Greatest of All Time. You will never, ever be forgotten. You and that love survives so we can rock forever on! I rock with you!"

482. "Gone but never forgotten! You are forever. The world is not enough!" A. Mays

483. "You will always be loved and remembered. We will miss U! Forever. D. Mont

484. "**R.I.P**. You were the best!" G.B.

485. "Remember the first time!"

486. "U are in a better place! Love you." Stella!!!

"OFF THE WALL SONNETS" FOR MICHAEL JACKSON

487. "**R.I.P**. **Michael**. I love you." A.S.

488. "Love **Michael**. **R.I.P**." Antonia

489. "Tovey Wall. **R.I.P**. **Mike**!"

490. "**R.I.P**. **Michael**. I love you!" A.S.

491. "We will miss you very much **Michael**. Love!" D. Sall

492. "JAMES, NY. LUV"

493.

"Off the Wall Sonnets" for Michael Jackson Photo.

FREDERICK MONDERSON
SENTIMENTS STATED BY NAME

I have tried to identify some names associated with Michael as indicated below given the times they were mentioned. Not all "categories" are listed and, sorry to say, sometimes I may be a bit off with the numbers.

Jackson – **20**

Michael – **116**

Mike – **23**

MJ – **52**

RIP – **119**

Rest in Peace – **20**

King of Pop – **17**

I Love You – **220**

Jackson Family – **7**

Forever – **16**

Greatest – **8**
Jesus, God Bless You – **6**

"OFF THE WALL SONNETS" FOR MICHAEL JACKSON

Black Man – **1**

Harlem – **2**

Heaven – **6**

Your Wife – **3**

"It's a complete lie, why do people buy these papers? It's not the truth I'm here to say. You know, don't judge a person, do not pass judgment, unless you have talked to them one on Children show me in their playful smiles the divine in everyone." **Michael Jackson**

3. MICHAEL JACKSON – ARCHANGEL

By

Dr. Fred Monderson

This inquiry and exposition is a rebuttal of the negativity that has attempted to drown the celebration of the life and work of the gifted and wonderful light Michael Jackson manifested and represented as an African American cultural phenomenon. In the continuum of attempting to degrade Black people one has to wonder whether the Media obsession with the flaws of this talented young man really reflects the toxic stream that runs in the American psycho-cultural consciousness.

The unfolding onslaught that has sought to tear down Mr. Jackson in life and now again in death, we saw in Byron Styron's depiction of Nat Turner, the revolutionary leader in 1831; with the attention paid the early heavyweight champion Jack Johnson; in the case against Marcus Garvey who founded the Universal Negro Improvement Association and who gave us the powerful symbol of the Red, Black and Green; and again with Paul Robeson, whose talents were on stage and screen, particularly on the international scene. Also, let us not forget what J. Edgar Hoover did to Dr. Martin Luther King as he waged the Civil Rights Struggle to help transform American society. Such Media assault efforts set out to upset the psychic equilibrium of these Black leaders and yet, after the sensational hounding, their names still-remained positively and indelibly imbedded in the collective consciousness of the African America community. This is so because, as Malcolm X instructed, "No matter what the man says, you better look into it." Therefore, and upon close inspection, it was revealed the full extent of the envy and vindictiveness contained in the Media onslaught. The only difference with Michael Jackson is that he was extraordinarily creative, yet tough, strong, and manifested tremendous good. Even more, he was bigger than all these leaders in that his contributions were national and international, in diverse fields. Still more, his giftedness was of a divinely inspired, magical, mystical spiritual nature so his creations soared heavenwards. Yet, in death, no compassion was shown in the Media frenzy now playing.

Nonetheless, those with the vision of consciousness realize Michael Jackson possessed and manifested the continuum of the artistic beauty of our people, the spiritual power, and the mysticism of the African, who from days of the plantation would sing:

"My lord what a morning when the stars begin to fall,
I've been buked and I've been scorned,
But I ain't going to lay my religion down."

Heaping buke and scorn on Brother Michael, not being mindful of his genius, in aid of sensationalism is simply shallow; still we will hold him high for beyond his many talents; he was an extraordinary humanitarian who sought to help and heal humanity. We must stand positively in solidarity with Michael Jackson! The media held Michael to a different standard, because they did not know him. And so, we will hold him high because there was much good in his actions. He changed popular culture by setting standards for people to come after him. He mirrored a sentiment of Malcolm X; 'The Man in the Mirror' is a powerful force for change. He is the leader we wait for; he encouraged us to empower ourselves wanting us to be compassionate towards humanity.

In all this, we cannot lose sight of the ancestral words of potent wisdom that has meant so much for, according to Dr. Leonard James of Stone Mountain, Georgia:

"Don't look for the flaws as you go through life
And even when you find them, it is wise
And it is kind to be somewhat blind
And look for the virtue behind them."

Therefore, the virtues of Brother Jackson far outweigh the flaws. This literary effort is therefore to correct an unfolding wrong, that is, to correct distortions and omissions systematically being implanted to destroy the name and legacy of Michael Jackson, because of his greatness. We know he was bigger than Elvis Presley and Frank Sinatra, perhaps better than both combined. Also, let's not forget Sammy Davis was better than most but did not get the recognition he deserved.

A legitimate question therefore is, 'how does Katherine Jackson in this time of grief feel about the negative publicity being showered on her beloved son?' This is a time of empathy and compassion for this gifted family, yet the media, viz., print, radio and television, fall tremendously short in this department. As such, when we consider this shoddy treatment, we are being reminded Michael Jackson and by extension the Jacksons are members of the American household, not members of the American family! Such a mindset is a throwback to the plantation mentality that wrecked so much psycho-social havoc on the African American family structure both physically and literally.

Nevertheless, in assessing this malady, 'let us not forget, all our dignity lies in thought, not in time and space which we cannot fill, therefore, let us endeavor to think well for that is the meaning of morality and spiritual power.'

In that universal humanistic outlook, we must remember John Dunn's immortal words:

"OFF THE WALL SONNETS" FOR MICHAEL JACKSON

"The death of any man diminishes me
For I am involved with humanity
Send not then for whom the bell tolls
For it tolls for thee!"

Thus, it must be pointed out, in the psychic consciousness of African-Americans the climb and the journey of Michael Jackson mirror our climb and journey on that steep hill in life. We must give Michael peace; he gave us peace, but did not get peace here on earth! Thank you Michael; rest peacefully; and may God bless your everlasting soul!

"Off the Wall Sonnets" for Michael Jackson Photo. Legendary Television newscaster holds photo of young Michael Jackson with his microphone sporting **Chanel 7**, New York, Logo.

"What one wishes is to be touched by truth and to be able to interpret that truth so that one may use what one is feeling and experiencing, be it despair or joy, in a way that will add meaning to one's life and will hopefully touch others as well."
Michael Jackson

4. MICHAEL JACKSON – BELOVED By Dr. Fred Monderson

The world was shocked at the untimely passing of Michael Jackson, singer, dancer, entertainer, humanitarian and as spontaneously electric as his music and performances have been, loyal and adoring fans took to the street at venues worldwide to honor the life's work and passing of an American icon, Elizabeth Taylor first dubbed the "King of Pop." From Presidents to Prisoners and Princes to Paupers, the explosive yet gentle giant was mourned for his lifelong contribution to the joyful exuberance of so many, for so long. Equally, in life as in death, media vultures continue to accentuate any human indiscretions Mr. Jackson may have been accused of, though in the eyes of the law he was found not guilty of criminal charges. Michael Jackson is not unlike so many creative, hardworking and oftentimes intellectually gifted blacks who must creatively perfect their craft, work hard to achieve a well-deserved acclaim, struggle to remain socially acceptable squeaky clean or brace for the unrelenting onslaught of perennial demonizing through the media's sensationalism. This therefore was the fate of the songbird Michael Jackson.

Fortunately, at this time especially fans do not wish to see their idol's name and memory further besmirched by critics fueled by envy and greed. The outpouring of affection for Mr.

Jackson and his family at this grievous time is a tremendous indication of people's long memory of the wonderful moments that Mr. Jackson has provided during their times of celebration of birthdays, weddings, graduations, at parties, concerts, driving to and from work, and any inconceivable number of times and was he provided sweet music that aided their joyous expressions.

Years ago, my mother, psychically talented, observing Michael Jackson performing on TV said, "When this young man dies the world will realize how creatively talented, mystical and spiritual he really was." She has been gone nearly 19 (35) years and now with his passing the-vast-majority of people will not only miss this musical genius but also realize there was something mystical, magical, and indeed spiritual about one who could reach so many, so far, in so many cultures across so many countries and continents. Truly, Michael Jackson's angelic voice seems fueled by divine inspiration proving a wonderful American cultural ambassador.

From the time of his passing, the outpouring of love and condolences to his family has shown Michael Jackson was beloved far and wide and the human frailties that marred the later ages of his wonderful career seemed inconsequential as fans celebrated his life, refusing to mourn the wonderful spirit they came to admire and love in the person of Michael Jackson. This creative genius was hard working, disciplined, a tremendous perfectionist who was truly international and a great musical star. He was a sensitive artistic genius who became vulnerable to vulturistic chicanery and so, out of fear became isolated and lonely. Yet he continued to create wonderful music that expressed the deepest sentiments of love and harmony that reflected the true genius of the man.

"Be humble, believe in yourself, and have the love of the world in your heart." **Michael Jackson**

5. The Staple Center Memorial to Michael Jackson on July 7, 2009.

The overhead banner read:

IN LOVING MEMORY

MICHAEL JACKSON

KING OF POP

1958-2009

The Michael Jackson memorial ceremony was one of the most watched events in history. It was probably only outdone by the Princess Diana funeral, but people from around the world were not as touched by the Princess as they were touched by Michael. So, while the "counters" say Michael's was viewed by 31 million viewers and the Princess 33 million, they were probably not counting the fact his tribute was carried live across the world. In the United States Michael's Memorial dominated the airwaves. TV Guide, New York 1, E!, CBS, TV One, NBC, ABC, Fox, Fox News, CNN, HLN, and MSNBC among others aired the proceedings. Radio stations probably were also involved. Almost all the TV stations did no commentary but simply let the uninterrupted show speak for itself.

By the time most of the guests were seated, the Andre Crouch Choir belted out "Going to see the King."

Smokey Robinson read **Tributes** from Diana Ross and Nelson Mandela.

Pastor Lucious Smith, family friend, described Michael Jackson as an

"Idol, Hero, even a king
Brother, son, father, friend,
Beloved part of Jesus, friend, and family of man

Remember the time
Gone too soon
Never really gone at all

Give love to the world
Moment of remembrance
Moment of healing
Moment of love.

Who is Diana Ross? Diana Ross has played an important part in the life of Michael Jackson, a sort of "other mother." She was with him from the beginning of his career, through the ups and downs and finally stood tall at the end. What a friendship. We first encounter their relationship when he was first introduced to the entertainment in:

Diana Ross Presents **The Jackson 5**

We see her again in the movie version of the show The Wiz.

At the end, overcome with emotion, she chose not to be at the Memorial but Diana Ross gave the first Tribute.

Paying the ultimate tribute to a lifelong friend, Michael Jackson chose to name Diana Ross in his Will to take care of his kids, in the event his beloved mother could not! He believed Diana Ross would take care of them as she had taken care of him. What love and confidence.

Michael Jackson was a student of music. He studied Tchaikovsky and Mozart. He also studied the dancing skills of Fred Astaire. Michael was ready and optimistic. He blended pyrotechnics, great dancing. To the question of 'Why his global impact?' The answer is simply the music. Music moves people. Michael was free, happy, optimistic, nice, a kind person and very polite.

The **Artists** who performed were Mariah Carey with Trey Lorenz who sang "I'll be there."

Lionel Ritchie sang "Jesus is Love."

Stevie Wonder "Never dreamed you'd leave in Summer." In opening he said, "This is a moment I wished I didn't live to see." He said further, as much as we may feel we need Michael here with us, God must have needed him more. I'm at peace with my love for Michael."

Jenifer Hudson did an outstanding rendition of "Will you be there?"

John Mayer performed "Human Nature" as an instrumental selection.

"OFF THE WALL SONNETS" FOR MICHAEL JACKSON

Jermaine Jackson performing "Smile."

Usher sang soulfully Michael you're "Gone Too Soon."

Shaheen Jafargholi of Britain's Got Talent sang "Who's Loving You?"

In closing, the Jackson Singers sang "We are the World" and "Heal the World."
All "We are the World."

Speakers were **Queen Latifah** who read a poem from Maya Angelou entitled "We Had Him!"

Berry Gordy, founder of Motown Records – In his tribute, Gordy said Michael Michael's "was like a son to me." He recalled, the "little kid had a quality I couldn't understand, but we all knew he was special." "His performance was well beyond his years. You could feel the happiness in his soul when he performed his songs. With Michael, the Jackson 5 were the only group in history to have their first four hits go to No. 1. In 1983 they reunited. Michael went into orbit and never came down. Michael Jackson accomplished everything he set out to do. At 10 years old he had passion to become the greatest entertainer in the world. He had 2 personalities. The soft spoken, childlike one and on stage, he was a master, take no prisoners showman. The King of Pop is not big enough. He is simply the greatest entertainer that ever lived. Thank you for the love. Thank you for the joy. You will always live in our hearts."

Kobe Bryant and Earvin "Magic" Johnson –

Kobe Bryant – "In the Guinness Book of World Records, Michael holds the record for most charities supported by a pop star."

Magic Johnson – "I saw the genius in Michael Jackson. He always had command of himself, the band and the audience. When I was invited to his home and order broiled chicken for dinner, Michael ordered Kentucky Fried Chicken. This is a celebration of his life, of his legacy. I want to thank Michael for keeping the doors open."

Rev. Al Sharpton called for "Love vigils to celebrate the life of a man who taught the world to love. Michael never let the world turn him around from his dream. He did not accept limitations. He did not accept limitations. He out sang his cynics. He outdistanced his doubters."

"It was Michael Jackson who brought Blacks, Asians, Latinos together. He fed the hungry before Live Aid and he created a comfort level. Kids from Japan, Ghana, France were dancing to his music. There's nothing that can't be don't if you put your mind to it. Michael was not about mess but about his message. He didn't love in vain." I want to say to his three children: There was nothing strange about your daddy. It was strange what he had to deal with.! But he dealt with it anyway. Come came here to say good bye, I came here to say Thank you. Thank You Michael. You never stopped. You never gave up. You broke down barriers. You gave us hope. Thank you. Thank you. Thank you."

Brooke Shields - "Michael was one of a kind. We enjoyed the most natural and easiest of friendships. We both understood what it was to be in the spotlight from a very young age. We laughed. Michael loved to laugh. Michael's laugh was the sweetest and purest of anyone I've known. He was a genius with unchallenged ability. He was honest, pure. He cared deeply for his friends, family and his fans. There was an extraordinary sensitivity about him. He looked with the heart. His favorite song was that written by Charlie Chaplin, 'Smile, though your heart is aching.' Somewhere up there he is perched on a crescent moon."

"OFF THE WALL SONNETS" FOR MICHAEL JACKSON

United States Representative Sheila Jackson Lee (D-Texas) also praised Michael Jackson for a life of constructive musical production.

Martin Luther King III and his sister Bernice King.

Martin Luther King III – "They say the sky's the limit, but Michael had no limit. You must discover your calling and be the best you can be. Michael Jackson was truly the best that he was. Martin Luther King did say do your job well, whether you were a doctor or street sweeper. Be the best you could be. Be the best street sweeper. On June 25, here on earth many did pause to say, Michael Joseph Jackson, here was a man who did all that he could to the best of his ability."

Bernice King – "My prayer is that no one fact or fiction can separate you from the love of God. Michael's life and work was inspired by the love of God."

Michael Ortega, Director of Michael Jackson Concert Tour. "We were here practicing. We knew we had to do this memorial here. This was to be his triumphant return to the world. This was his best work. "

Germaine Jackson – "I would like to thank everyone for coming out. We thank you. We thank you. We thank you."

Marlon – "We are trying to understand why the Lord has taken our brother. Michael, when you left us a part of me went with you. I will treasure the fun we had singing, dancing, dancing and mother would say boys it's time to go to the recording studio. Despite your disguises, you're my brother, I can spot you anywhere. You wore a crown, you were judged, ridiculed. Maybe now they will leave you alone. Michael was the voice of our angelic trumpet. Whenever we parted and I said I love you, he would say "I love you more." Your ultimate reward is in the lord's presence. I thank you. I thank you. When you get to heaven, give my brother Brandon, my twin, a hug."

Paris, **Michael's daughter** – "From the time I was born, Daddy has been the best father you can ever imagine. I just want to say I love him very much."

Janet – "Thank you for loving our brother. Thank you. Good night."

Pastor Lucious Smith closed with the **Benediction**. He explained: "All around us are people of different cultures, different religions, different nationalities. And yet, the music of Michael Jackson brings us together."

While the above performers were clearly visible on stage, it's expected the Staples Center was laden with other celebrities. Various news services gave the names of the following celebrities: Cicely Tyson, P. Diddy, Rick, Kathy and Nicky Hilton, Lil Kim, Chris Brown, Mickey Rooney, Tatum O'Neal.

Emotions probably overcame Quincy who was quoted as saying, "I can't attend any more funerals" and Elizabeth Taylor who wanted to mourn Michael in private.

"OFF THE WALL SONNETS" FOR MICHAEL JACKSON

"Off the Wall Sonnets" for Michael Jackson Photo. Little Richard, "Mr. Give it My All" on stage. "Follow the Golden Rule. Be kind to your neighbors, love them as much as you would love yourself, do unto others." **Michael Jackson**

6. BEATING BACK WOLVES AT THE DOOR

By

Dr. Fred Monderson

In death as in life, Michael Jackson's image remains tarnished in the Media as it appears, which cannot say a positive word, for as Rev Al Sharpton said, "Why harp on the negative, why not ask questions about the positive things the man has done?"

The Media's obsession with whether Michael Joseph Jackson used drugs or harping on claims of sexual misconduct seems to underscore, at this historically important time, going 'up the down staircase' or 'driving in the wrong direction on a one way street. The people whom Michael Jackson reached, those touched by his music, his adorable fans, people in the music industry-influenced by him and are carrying forth his legacy, are determined at this time that "good will triumph over evil," and Michael Jackson will get his due!

When questioned about burials in the African American tradition, **Professor John Henrik Clarke** replied, "We put them away nicely!" This is what those who love him in the Civil Rights Movement, entertainment, the clergy and adoring fans worldwide are striving sternly to accomplish!

Now, as I stumble through the morass of allegations against Michael Jackson following his death, I remained convinced this wonderful soul is a victim of innuendos, speculations, lies, ignorance, and "matchstick men mentalities" and those who tried to swindle the entertainer. We are all familiar with the role of the Media in the constant replay of innuendos and false claims to nauseating proportions.

The Cable station CNN reported on July 6th, 2009, on Wolf Blitzer's Situation Room Ticker that Rep. King said "There is nothing good about this guy!" Imagine! Michael Jackson holds the Guinness Book World Record for charity giving somewhere between 300-500 million US Dollars. This man only bears the name King which he was born with. Through hard work, dedication and creativity Michael Jackson earned the title "King of Popular culture music." This is a global acclimation and one billion people worldwide watched the Staples Center memorial in Los Angeles! There is only one King of New York, that person is Rev. Al Sharpton. Instead of spending time saying scurrilous things about Mr. Michael Jackson, Mr. Peter King should be more concerned whether this is his last term as a Congressman from New York, since he is on the Democratic Radar Screen to be defeated at the next Congressional election. His colleagues in the House of Representatives honored Michael Jackson with a moment of silence. One has-to wonder what he was doing when they were so acting. Equally, President Obama praised Mr. Jackson as "one of the greatest entertainers of our time." He was in good stead with American Presidents Nixon and Reagan, with foreign royalty and enjoyed a fan-base in every country across the globe.

This is why the attitude and posturing of Rep. King, himself a loser, is exactly symptomatic of the adherents of "Jackson character assassination" based on rumors and innuendos fed by Media power and influence. As a result, the false claims against Mr. Jackson have taken on a life of its own. Another example of the perennial "black balling of Mr. Jackson" has to do with the claims of his prescription drug use. Rush Limbaugh is a reported drug addict, prescription drug addict, but no one is going after him, because he is not black! Imagine, news reporters were tracking down leads that Mr. Jackson had used such medication in 1996. Imagine! Again!

Wolf Blitzer on CNN's Situation Room, July 6, 2009, 4:00-7:00 pm, interviewed Mr. Tom Mesereau who defended Michael Jackson in the child molestation trial. Mr. Mesereau said, according to his research Mr. Jackson "was never a child molester; he was a wonderful person!" The attorney talked about how Michael was "acquitted 14 times, 10 felonies and 4 misdemeanors." Then he went into how the District Attorney brought 4 witnesses to testify against Michael, who in fact, said "he had never molested or done anything inappropriate with them." The Prosecution's witnesses became character witnesses for Michael. The millions of kids who passed through Neverland and they could only find 4 who could not support the Prosecution's case. Mr. Mesereau next discussed how the accuser and his brother were discredited through inconsistencies in their statements. Next Mr. Blitzer brought up the fact Mr. Jackson had settled a suit, in the past, for millions of dollars when the charge of child molestation was brought against him. This is when Mr. Mesereau pointed out Michael Jackson was surrounded by "mediocre people who did not have his best interest at heart."

When the money grab was made, these people whom we can generally equate with parasites, are the one who suggested such "accusations would not look good for Mr. Jackson's image." This is when they all agreed to pay the "go away money" in a settlement thinking the issue would go away. However, this was the first of the one-two punch to derail his creatively cultural express and destroy Mr. Jackson himself.

In the movie Malcolm X, directed by Spike Lee and starring Denzel Washington, the scene is in front of the police station after the Muslim brother was arrested and held in the precinct. The Muslim brothers gathered, Malcolm arrived, with hand gestures he communicated with the phalanx of disciplined black men who appeared willing to do anything Minister Malcolm pronounced, even storming the precinct. When the police Captain observed the unfolding phenomenon taking place in front of him he turned to one of his Lieutenants and confessed, "That Negro has too much power!" Therein lay the fear that motivates people to attempt to destroy Michael Jackson the successfully powerful black man.

While some have argued Malcolm X was radical, Michael Jackson's power was in his creative gentility and artistic genius ability. That artistic creativity was fueled and fired ostensibly by divine guidance and inspiration. This gift bred a consciousness to empathize with the sufferings of humanity and through the soothing potency of song and dance; Jackson hoped to impart a message of healing through expressions of love and giving. Let us not forget, two thousand years ago, another gentle soul, proponent of love, healing and giving was crucified by similar "wolves at the door" as the ones who hounded Michael Jackson in life and death.

Next, having beaten back the child molestation accusations as represented in the charges, Mr. Mesereau was questioned about drug use by Michael to which he responded, Mr. Jackson never appeared impaired in any way during any time they were in contact. He was always consciously consistent. This was a man in complete control of his faculties. Finally,

"OFF THE WALL SONNETS" FOR MICHAEL JACKSON

Wolf posed the money question, whether Mr. Jackson had paid for his services. Mr. Mesereau responded, "Michael was very good to us." This is why this is "a very, very sad moment" for those who loved and cared about him.

Such contentions are somewhat reminiscent of Rev. Al Sharpton's Apollo Theater and Post-Apollo Memorial pronouncement that "Michael's image was tarnished by the Media." He said, "Wait a minute, people loved Michael, they knew him and respected him. Michael Jackson was a forerunner for Tiger Woods, Oprah Winfrey, and Barack Obama. His fame was based on talent. He created a comfort level that expressed a positive view. Michael Jackson is a strong historic force being treated unfairly. We believe in him and that is why we stand up for Michael Jackson."

"Off the Wall Sonnets" for Michael Jackson Photo. Gently laying down gifts of love for a loving, departed soul.

This gentle soul was an iconic figure. He was kind, well-spoken, well-read, giving, and a loving father as well as a global superstar. This loving, caring, transformational figure is, as Ossie Davis said of Malcolm, "he was our Prince, Our Shining Black Prince!" That is why at 5:26 pm (EST) (2:26 PST) on Tuesday, June 30, 2009, inside the Apollo, five days to the minute after Michael passed, Al Sharpton, before calling for a moment of silence for Michael Jackson, said to the Media, "You can lie on him, we stand up for him. We are here to preserve his legacy with dignity. His work, his life, his dignity must be preserved, because he was a wonderful man who was smeared in life and death." There are many who will not stand for any form of assault on the character, creative intellectual abilities and giving nature of our heroes and especially when their lives are devoted to improving the good of humanity in general.

"Off the Wall Sonnets" for Michael Jackson Photo. Michael often voiced his love for the fans, and they too often returned the sentiment as this beauty is here doing.

"OFF THE WALL SONNETS" FOR MICHAEL JACKSON

"Being on stage is magic. There's nothing like it. You feel the energy of everybody who's out there, you feel it all over your body. When the lights hit you, it's all over, I swear it is."
Michael Jackson

7. JOE JACKSON
By
Dr. Fred Monderson

Mr. Joseph Jackson, father of Michael Jackson, is a parent reviled by the media because he did not fulfill their ideal of how a man should raise his children. Afterall, isn't the final product the best barometer of how well one has done in a particular task. Take for instance, Mr. William, father of Venus and Serena Williams, tennis phenoms who have excelled in that sport. He has come in for his share of criticisms because he does not fit the mold. Yet, he produced two world class daughters and while not controversial, they were certainly successfully trained, driven and accomplished acclaimed heights. Mr. Jackson's handiwork produced equally astonishing results, if not more so, in that all the members of his family became successful entertainers.

With the passing of Michael, Mr. Joe Jackson's presence at the Black Entertainment Television tribute was criticized and again in the news conference with Rev. Al Sharpton the critics continued their assault. Apparently, Mr. Jackson began pedaling on **BET's** red carpet a new record company he was forming and again with Rev. Al Sharpton he had to again explain he was grieving inside. The critics, both professional and lay, complained this was an inappropriate time for Mr. Jackson to be pitching his new company. However, objectively speaking, it was the appropriate time to make such an announcement.

When we consider how the entertainment and entrepreneurial wolves have swooped down and began exploiting the name, life's work and legacy of Michael Jackson for personal gain; Joe Jackson, as a seasoned musical campaign insider wanted to convey the unmistakable message that there would be no music vacuum created by Michael's passing. In fact, he wanted to establish continuity in his family remaining in the music business.

We need to understand Mr. Joe Jackson's history, for at 80 years old, he is a child of the Great depression, too young to serve in World War II but certainly the Korean Conflict. Equally, as Mr. Jackson matured in the pre-Civil Rights age he had to confront American society's racism and challenges to the black family. Yet Mr. Joseph Jackson was lucky to find a job as a steel worker, meet the beautiful Katherine, marry and begin raising a family. Thus, the credible questions should surround what types of experiences he confronted in his many travels and travails and what shaped the determination his family would not share the same experiences.

Upon realizing he had talented kids, Joe began cultivating their musical skills and insisting hard work was essential. The old adage, 'How do you get to Carnegie Hall? You practice, practice, practice' became the watchword for the ultimate success Joe envisioned. Subsequently as the Jackson family became renowned for their musical talents, in an interview on Oprah Winfrey show, Michael Jackson was heard to say his father whipped him and forced him to practice unending. Therein lay the charges that Joe Jackson was an unfit father because he disciplined his child. Therefore, here lay the crux of the matter that perhaps painted an incorrect portrait of a father whose concerns were misunderstood.

That interview in this enlightened age of corporal punishment and avoidance ought not to be applied to Joe Jackson for it undermines his parenting skills and-also his concern for his family. The society condemns absentee fathers, which Mr.

"OFF THE WALL SONNETS" FOR MICHAEL JACKSON

Jackson was not. Today we insist you not discipline your child, but with all the distractions and inducements children very easily are led astray. In those cases, law enforcement does discipline them and with behaviors bordering on brutality and a prison industrial complex that threatens and destroys their manhood, physically, emotionally and psychologically. All this notwithstanding, many older persons will gladly confess their parents took the rod to them and they came out pretty-well. Now as the law emphasizes non-corporal punishment, seems those with limited education and resources are caught unprepared to be "good parents," then their children get into trouble.

Sure Mr. Jackson ran a tight ship, he was tough on his children, he was not absent, he was strict and lo and behold, when we consider the results of his insistence, Mr. Michael Jackson became a wonderful success as did many of his siblings. As an extension of the argument, an artist, a painter, sees, envisions and paints a picture, not as the viewing public sees it but as he envisioned the image he hopes to create. Joe Jackson, in vowing to make his son a superstar never envisioned the Oprah Winfrey interview. If his methods had been different, there probably would not have been such an interview that followed the trail of success leading to it.

"Off the Wall Sonnets" for Michael Jackson Photo. James Brown, "The Godfather of Soul!"

"I think that God makes everything 100 percent. So, if you don't like it, blame God." **Michael Jackson**

8. THE BODY OF WORK (Partial)

1.	I Want You back.	1969
2.	Who's Loving You.	1969
3.	I'll Be There.	1970
4.	ABC.	1970
5.	Mama's Pear.	1971
6.	Don't Stop Til You Get Enough.	1979
7.	Rock With You.	1979
8.	Billy Jean	1982
9.	Wanna Be Startin Something	1983
10.	Human Nature	1983
11.	Thriller	1984
12.	The Way You Make Me Feel	1987
13.	Smooth Criminal	1988
14.	Man in the Mirror	1988
14.	Black or White	1991
15.	Scream	1995

"Off the Wall Sonnets" for Michael Jackson Photo.

"OFF THE WALL SONNETS" FOR MICHAEL JACKSON

"Off the Wall Sonnets" for Michael Jackson Photo. "Teddies for Mike!"

"In their innocence, children offer a lesson to adults: to be spontaneous, genuine, and free of superficiality." **Michael Jackson**

9. THE MICHAEL JACKSON TIMELINE By Dr. Fred Monderson

It is difficult to sketch a timeline about the fascinating experiences Michael Jackson was part of from the time of his first singing outing with a band formed by his brothers and supervised by his father Joseph, a former musician turned steelworker. Information provided for this timeline is provided by *USA Today* Special Edition; The New York *Daily News* "Jackson: A life in the spotlight" by Patrick Huguenin and Gina Salamone, Friday, June 26, 2009, pp. 41-43. In addition, Brooks Barnes's "Jackson's Estate: Piles of Assets, Loads of Debt" *New York Times*, Saturday, June 27, 2009, p. A 11, also provided information for this timeline.

August 29, 1958 – Michael Jackson is born to Joseph and Katherine Jackson

1965 – 7-year-old Michael joins a band formed by his brothers Jermaine, Tito and Jackie Jackson. Marlon also becomes a member of the band.

1966 – 8-year-old Michael and his brothers wins a talent show at Roosevelt High school in Gary, Indiana. Then they begin to play across the state and in Chicago before touring across the country.

1967 and 1968 - The Jackson Five 5 release two of their first singles you don't have to be 21 to fall in love and Big Boy. In 1968 they appear at the Apollo Theater Amateur Show in Harlem, New York. Gladys Knight and the Pips recognize their talent and recommend them to Barry Gordon, founder of Motown Records. Soon the group produced four No. 1 hits, "I want you back," "ABC," "The love you save," and "I'll be there."

1969-1970 – The Jackson 5 were the feature on the "Ed Sullivan Show"

1971 –

1972 –

"OFF THE WALL SONNETS" FOR MICHAEL JACKSON

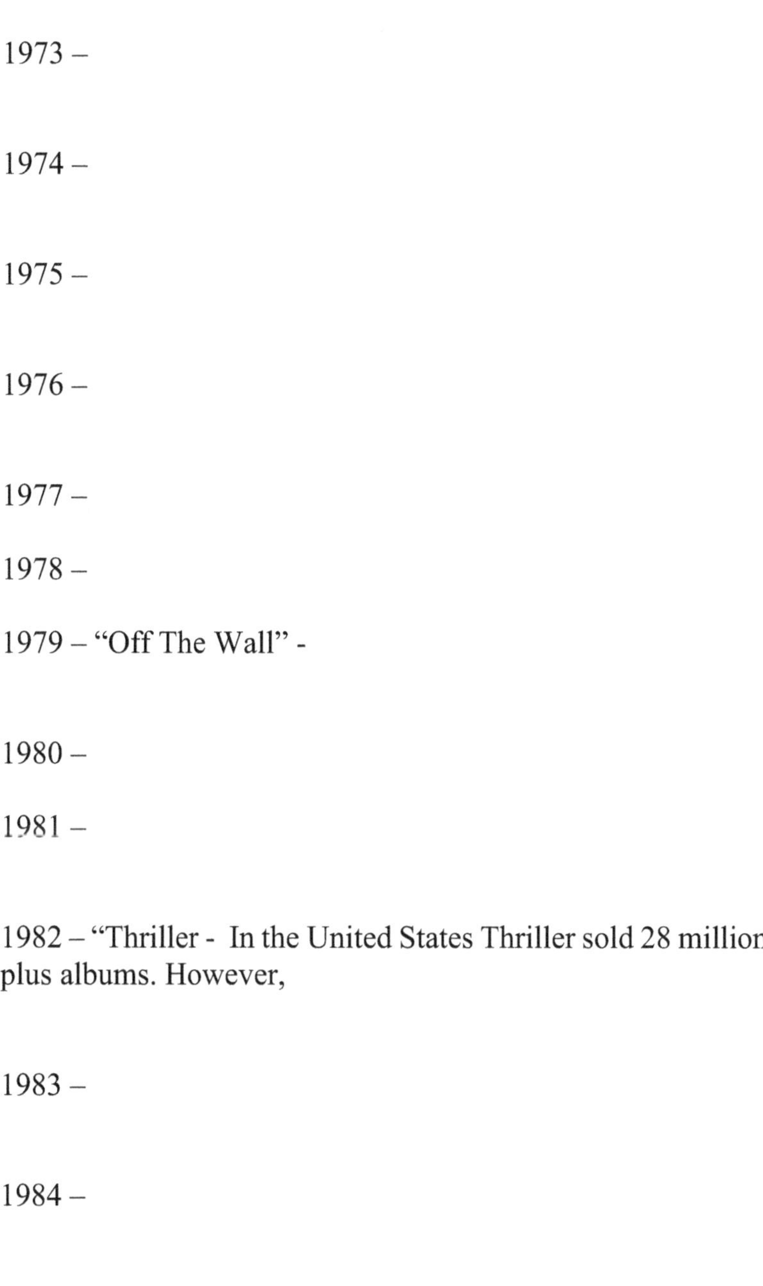

1973 –

1974 –

1975 –

1976 –

1977 –

1978 –

1979 – "Off The Wall" -

1980 –

1981 –

1982 – "Thriller - In the United States Thriller sold 28 million plus albums. However,

1983 –

1984 –

1985 – Michael Jackson purchases the Beatles Catalogue for an estimated $47.5 million. Today it is worth close to one billion dollars. Some believe purchasing this Catalogue and marrying Lisa Marie Prestley were the sources for much of the enmity directed towards Mr. Jackson.

1986 –

1987 – "Bad" - Martin Scorsese produced a video for the album at a cost of approximately $1million.

1988 – Mr. Jackson purchased a 2600-acre ranch to create Neverland, a play place for kids, reminisce of Peter Pan's famous place. He spent some $35 million to outfit it with a zoo, amusement park, and 50-seat theater. In 1999 he reported it cost $5million to operate the play-land annually.

1990 –

1991 – "Dangerous"

1992 –

1993 – Word is now out that Mr. Jackson was pressured

1994 –

1995 – "HIStory: Past, Present and Future Book I"

1996 –

1997 – "Blood on the Dance Floor: History in the Mix" -

"OFF THE WALL SONNETS" FOR MICHAEL JACKSON

1998 –

1999 –

2000 –

2001 – "Invincible" -

2002 –

2003 – "Number Ones" -

2004 –

2005 –

2006 –

2007 –

2008 –

2009 –

"Off the Wall Sonnets" for Michael Jackson Photo. Aretha Franklin, "The Queen of Soul!"

"If you enter this world knowing you are loved and you leave this world knowing the same, then everything that happens in between can be dealt with." **Michael Jackson**

10. PRESIDENTS TO PRISONERS SALUTE MICHAEL JACKSON

It's a known fact Presidents Richard Nixon and Ronald Reagan admire and recognized Michael Jackson as a musical and artistic genius. This was particularly so of Ronald Reagan, the actor who easily recognized Michael's talents. The Bushes, certainly young George and especially the "party animal" Bill Clinton would have danced to Michael's soulfully rhythmic and titillating music. While Jimmy Carter may have been somewhat reserved, Andrew Young in the Cabinet may have insisted a Jackson number or two be spin at one of the celebrations.

Since young people loved Michael Jackson, President Carter's daughter Amy may certainly have played either the Jackson 5 or Michael's records at her birthday parties in the White House. It is not inconceivable that Barack Obama, while out "sowing his royal oats" whether at Columbia or Harvard would have danced to Michael Jackson, the hottest entertainer of the age, not realizing one day he would end up being the first African American President. Therefore, in his comments upon Michael's passing, the President praised Mr. Jackson as being the greatest entertainer of our time, though he was not unmindful of the tragedies of this man's life.

During the good times when Michael was topping the charts, America not only loved him but also relished in him as American ambassador of goodwill exporting American culture through his music. During these good times Michael Jackson was the guest wined and dined by the princes and cultural royalty of the great houses on all the continents who chose to be with and be seen with the icon musical "royalty," King of Popular culture. But, while Michael enjoyed the hospitality of global royalty, he was not unmindful of the plight of paupers and, as such, he devoted large sums of his fortune and made special efforts to aid the less fortunate. His humanitarian nature and efforts to help the less fortunate are renowned. His charity work preceded "Live Aid" and "We are the world" productions and innumerable charitable organizations he supported. The United Negro College Fund was a particular beneficiary of his generosity. As in life, so in death, his will states, portions of his wealth will continue to benefit charities.

Where money was not given, the image and musical genius and influence of the great artist, who performed with passion and electricity, reached into the prisons with a therapeutic effect. More than a year ago, prison authorities in the Philippines launched an innovative dance program to motivate and rehabilitate its inmates. With skepticism the world viewed this new approach to rehabilitate, some even scoffing at it. When U-Tube picked it up and it appeared a sensation on the internet and elsewhere, there was something to this became a popular refrain. With Michael Jackson's passing, emotions overwhelmed and the Philippines prisoners were the first to pay homage to their hero whose songs were inspirational and enabled them to emotionally empower themselves through dance as a part of something bigger than themselves in a disciplined and constructive manner. Here is another example of Michael Jackson's influence that did not involve money, yet, has produced a long-lasting result that moved these people to a higher plane of emotional and artistic consciousness.

"Off the Wall Sonnets" for Michael Jackson Photo. Classic MJ amidst the platitudes of fans!

Score another positive and constructive contribution for Michael Jackson whose humanistic path is strewn with many such, even unintentional successes in his effort to share love, help heal humanity and bring out the best in people. Truly, Michael Jackson was a great soul, imbued with the spark of divinity, all doing the Lord's work!

"OFF THE WALL SONNETS" FOR MICHAEL JACKSON

"I'm a black American, I am proud of my race. I am proud of who I am. I have a lot of pride and dignity." **Michael Jackson**

11. EXPRESSING THE VOICE OF THE PEOPLE

Dr. Fred Monderson

Teddy Cubia, June 25, 2009, retired New York City Educator believed: "These are the highest events of our lifetime; the birth of the first Black President and the death of a musical icon, Barack Obama and Michael Jackson."

According to **Mr. Cubia**, "Michael represented the epitome of artistry, so classic with his style that he transcended the entertainment industry in every ethnic denomination."

Cubia further believed, "Claims of parental misconduct are unfounded. Michael never really grew up. Joe was very strict in his discipline. He wanted to make his diamond in the rough shine. Joe believed and reinforced the notion; the quickest way to Carnegie Hall is rehearse. Joe disciplined Michael to the elements of artistry to perfection."

Quincy Jones – June 25, 2009 – "I am absolutely devastated at this tragic and unexpected news. I've lost my little brother today and part of my soul has gone with him."

Tommy Mottola, for mer head of Sony Music – June 25, 2009 – Mr. Jackson was "the cornerstone to the entire music business. He bridged the gap between the rhythm and blues and pop music and made it into a global culture."

Doris Darrington (77) of Gary, Indiana – June 26, 2009 – "Has always been a source of pride for Gary, even though he wasn't around much. The older person, that's not the Michael we knew. We knew the little bitty boy with the big Afro and the brown skin. That's how I'll always remember Michael."

Tiffany Howard of Brooklyn, in the New York *Daily News* Saturday, June 27, 2009, under Voice of the People: Mourning Michael wrote: "Words can't describe "The Way You Make Me Feel,: You made me feel like a "P.Y.T," even though you never said my name the way you did "Billie Jean," You said I was "The Lady in Your Life," and with those words, "You Rock My World." You knew it was "Human Nature" to "Wanna Be Startin' Something" because you were "Bad" – but a "Smooth Criminal." And they would never "Beat It" and "Leave you Alone." Your music helped "Heal the World" in so many ways. That's why we will forever "Jam" and "Rock With You," even until the "Break of Dawn." You'll be remembered as a true "Dancing Machine," a "Thriller," a legend in your own time who has "Gone Too Soon." I hope you know "I just Can't Stop Loving You."

Errol Lewis columnist of the *Daily News* in "What Michael meant to me" *Daily News* Sunday, June 29, 2009, p. 27, wrote: Michael Jackson first entered show business as the youngest product of the Motown record label, a legendary pop-culture juggernaut that had already launched the likes of Marvin Gaye, the Supremes, Stevie Wonder, and the Temptations. Toiling under the watchful eye of Motown founder Berry Gordy, a team of producers and songwriters called The Corporation scripted the look and sound of what they dubbed "Bubblegum soul." They took the Motown formula – teen music whose rugged gospel and blues roots were blended with stripes, do-wop harmony and bright, catchy hooks – and made it kid-friendly...."

"OFF THE WALL SONNETS" FOR MICHAEL JACKSON

"And by the time we were full grown, Michael was swimming in the deep currents of American musical genius. His groundbreaking solo album, "Off the Wall," was produced by Quincy Jones – a dazzling composer/arranger who'd started as a young trumpeter in the Dizzy Gillespie Band...."

"Off the Wall Sonnets" for Michael Jackson Photo. Males, like Michael Jackson, do adore baskets of flowers!

"When all is said and done, Michael's trials and tribulations, the snide recitations of court cases and financial woes, will amount to no more than trivia. Michael Jackson and the music he made are baked into too many lives, minds and hearts to be anything but a glorious legend in the end – one that will live well beyond my lifetime and yours."

Mike Jaccarino Constant "paint part of his life" in **Daily News** Sunday, June 28, 2009, p. 6, quoted R. Kelly who expressed his sympathy in the following: "I am truly saddened that my mentor, brother and friend will no longer be with us physically. At the same time, I feel so blessed to have been touched by his music, his dance, his lyrics and his pure genius. It is because of Michael's yesterday that I am who I am today."

Jan Ransom and Bill Hutchinson with Tanyanika Samuels "The Apollo launches tributes" *Daily News*, Sunday, June 28, 2009, p. 5, quoted Rev. Al Sharpton: "He was the king of popular culture and I'm not going to let them reduce Michael to some king of freak show... but Michael was a true genius. To create music that outsold any other artist in his generation, can't no freak do that."

Even further the columnists wrote, "Vendors lining the sidewalk across the street from the Apollo were doing brisk business hawking Jackson CDs, DVDs, posters, photos, and T-shirts. Nova Selder, 31, of Queens said he sold five-dozen Jackson videos at $15 apiece on Thursday and had sold out of CDs he was offering for $5 each. 'People are buying it, buying it, buying it,' Selder said."

Tanyanika Samuels "Rev. Al vows to fight for Michael" in *Daily News* Sunday, June 28, 2009, p. 5, quoted Rev. Al Sharpton: "'If we can look past the shortcomings of Frank Sinatra and Elvis Presley, then we can put into proper perspective any shortcomings Michael may have had,' he said. Sharpton said he knew Jackson was at peace. 'When you get to heaven,' he said, looking skyward, 'turnaround and moonwalk through the gates.'"

Venues for watching the event as shown on the TV screen included: London, Berlin, New Delhi, Harlem, New York, Raleigh, North Carolina, First AME Church of Los Angeles, Times square, New York on a Jumbo-tron, the Staples Center, Los Angeles, Neverland ranch, Gary Indiana, Atlanta, Hollywood, Las Vegas. In fact, people around the world watched this historic Home Going ceremony for Michael Jackson.

On **LARRY KING LIVE** July 7, 2009, 9:00-10:00 pm, Dionne Warwick and her son appeared.

On Larry King Twitter, as shown on the TV screen:

EJay – "An excellent home going for Michael."

Rohan – "Michael Jackson was the MAN and thes best entertainer."

Angela – "Michael's costumes should be on display at Neverland."

Fran – "Michael Jackson was not just an icon, but a genius with a message."

Brown – "Michael Jackson set the bar for songs, videos and fashion."

Judy – "Michael Jackson was a great entertainer who did a lot for AIDS and other causes."

Matt – "Michael was an icon of our time, only Elvis was comparable."

Afrida – "Michael was the best entertainer, musician and humanitarian."

Maria – "King of pop and his music and videos will last forever."

Vincent – "Michael Jackson will never die. He will live on in his music."

Lynn – "Michael will live on in his children and Neverland."

Deanna – "I hope Michael gets the peace he never did in life."

Gotham Chopra – Michael's funeral was "very elegant and dignified."

Rose – "Michael's abilities opened the door for African American artists".

Brian – "Michael gave up his life and money everything for people."

Charmichael – "It takes a lot for me to cry. I haven't stopped."

Patti Austin – "Michael studied the greats who came before him."

L.H. "Michael, the man with a platinum soul."

Rohan Lisa – "Neverland should be owned by one of Michael's charities."

"OFF THE WALL SONNETS" FOR MICHAEL JACKSON

Roxanne – "Michael was a gift to the world."

Al Sharpton on Anderson Cooper AC 360, CNN, July 7, 2009, 10: 00-12:00 pm – "Michael kept going. He did not accept limitations. Michael broke down the color curtain. He brought together Black, white, Asian, Latino. He outperformed the pessimists. Michael Never stopped. Michael Never stopped; Michael Never stopped."

"The whole service was almost flawless. He was the one, MTV and Rolling stone put on their cover. He helped create the culture of comfort. He brought changes to your eyes, your biases, your fears. His children were in a web of love."

"Off the Wall Sonnets" for Michael Jackson Photo. Chuck Jackson, "What a scintillating voice!"

"The meaning of life is contained in every single expression of life. It is present in the little things that are everything. It is the music of the universe in the smallest humming of the wind. It is the incredible wood grain pattern in the table you are sitting at." **Michael Jackson**

12. COMMENTATORS ON MICHAEL JACKSON

Donna Brazile, the Democratic strategist and CNN Commentator mentioned Michael's music, movements and his humanitarianism. He stretched "Hands Across America" and was instrumental in "Live Aid" and "We are the world" which was done with Lionel Ritchie. Michael Jackson was dancing and celebrating life itself." Donna thought the Memorial, "an organized event. It was a celebration of his life, work, legacy. Many charities will continue to benefit from his legacy."

Michael Jackson was huge in the United States but massive abroad. In his spectacular 'We are the world' this is the first time that many entertainers worked together. Michael gave tremendously to charity. He supported the United Negro College Fund. He is reported as giving anywhere from 300 to 500 million dollars to charity. The children gave his life new meaning. His hat (fedora), glove, jacket, socks, black pants were his singular trademark. There were many Michaels for many souls. There was universal love and respect for his music."

Roland Martin, a syndicated Radio Host and CNN Host and Commentator reflected on the somber celebration given to Michael Jackson. He stated in the Black community, the tradition is one of a "Home Going Service." Mr. Martin thought Michael is now "In a better place. He will have no more pain. No more sorrow. No more heartache. There will be no more tortured challenges. Michael loved to perform. There were never any shifting attitudes for Michael in the African American community. African Americans adored Michael because of his music."

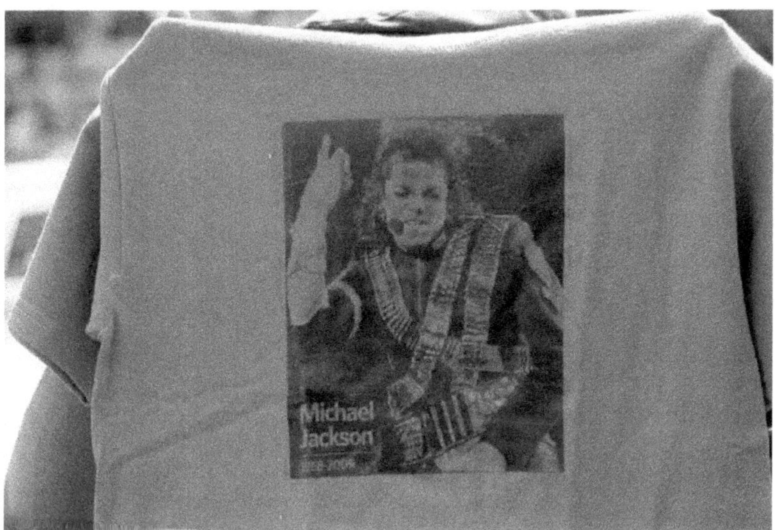

"Off the Wall Sonnets" for Michael Jackson Photo. The "King of Pop" in action!

"Off the Wall Sonnets" for Michael Jackson Photo. The crown trying to view the "Idol in confetti!"

"Off the Wall Sonnets" for Michael Jackson Photo. Michael was for the people, and the people came out for Michael.

"OFF THE WALL SONNETS" FOR MICHAEL JACKSON

"I'm starting with the man in the mirror / I'm asking him to change his ways / And no message could have been any clearer/ If you wanna make the world a better place / Take a look at yourself and then make a change." **Michael Jackson**

13. VISCERAL CONCERN By Dr. Fred Monderson

Visceral Concern: Since the death of Michael Jackson, establishment Media has used power and influence to defame this great artist and to diminish his legacy and his value to the Black Community and to the world.

PURPOSE: The purpose of this brief inquiry is to:

1. Establish or deny the authenticity of the negative innuendos and rumors pertaining to Michael Jackson.

2. To assert the inescapable contribution this brother has made not only to the performing arts but to the positive imagery of American culture worldwide.
3. Donna Brazile reminded, Michael was big at home but massive abroad.

My hypothesis is therefore interrogative, which states:

Is there substantive evidence in the record to support the proposition that Michael Jackson was subjected to parental abuse which primarily led to patterns of behavior that were non-traditional and whether this has led to his dependence on narcotics. The Methodological Tools to be utilized will include:

1. Historical Outline
2. Cause and Effect
3. Comparison and Contrast
4. Systematic Conceptual Scheme of Analysis and this requires:

    a. Purpose
    b. Concepts selected must have relevance
    c. They must be Precise
    d. They must contain bases for problem solving theory

5. Concepts:

    a. Parental Responsibilities
    b. Talent
    c. Internal Interactions

        i. Father
        ii. Mother
        iii. Family

    d. External Interactions and influences

        i. Barry Gordy
        ii. Diana Ross
        iii. James Brown
        iv. Media
        v. Jessie Jackson
        vi. Al Sharpton

6. Critical Summary:

        i. Parental Responsibility to maximize the potential of a child. Did Jackson's parents do this?
        ii. Siblings influences and interactions
        iii. Matrimonial Relations and his children

"OFF THE WALL SONNETS" FOR MICHAEL JACKSON

iv. People whose financial lifeblood depended on Michael Jackson

a. The Music Industry with its:
Producers
Directors
Distributors
Musicians
Audience
Intra/Inter group relations (race)

v. Charitable Contributions

a. National
b. International

7. Interpretative Summary

8. The Body of Work

9. The Michael Jackson Legacy

10. What people are saying

"Off the Wall Sonnets" for Michael Jackson Photo. Throngs of fans flocked to Harlem to pay tribute the deceased musical genius.

"Consciousness expresses itself through creation. This world we live in is the dance of the creator. Dancers come and go in the twinkling of an eye but the dance lives on. On many an occasion when I am dancing, I have felt touched by something sacred. In those moments, I felt my spirit soar and become one with everything that exists." Michael Jackson

14. Michael Jackson in Retrospect

The death of Michael Jackson shocked the world but more important it shocked some individuals into realizing that life is indeed fragile, tender, even precious and sometimes short. Nevertheless, a philosophical belief holds, "It's not how long you live, but what you do while on earth and what is your legacy." Another somewhat mundane belief is "you come into this world crying, structure your life so that when you depart people will cry because you represent a loss." To both of these admonitions, Michael Jackson is a perfect example of one whose legacy is assured and with tumultuous tears shed at his passing, he will surely be missed!

Michael Jackson was born to Joseph and Katherine Jackson in Gary, Indiana, on August 29, 1958. The second youngest, his male siblings were Jackie, Tito, Jermaine, Marlon and Randy. The twin of Marlon, Brandon, died and in his tribute to his brother asked Michael to give him a hug when he got to heaven. The sisters were Rebbie, La Toya and Janet. Brooks Barnes' "A Star Idolized and Haunted, Michael Jackson Dies at 50" in *New York Times*, Friday, June 26, 2009, Cover and pages A22-23, writes about the family and that: "They all survive him, as do his parents Joseph and Katherine Jackson, of Las Vegas, and three children: Michael Joseph Jackson, Jr., Paris Michael Katherine Jackson, born to Mr. Jackson's second wife Deborah Jeanne Rowe, and Prince Michael Joseph II, the son of a surrogate mother. Mr. Jackson was briefly married to Lisa Marie Prestley, the daughter of Elvis Prestley.

"OFF THE WALL SONNETS" FOR MICHAEL JACKSON

7

"Off the Wall Sonnets" for Michael Jackson Photo. More of the people, this time inside the Apollo Theater.

Michael began performing with four brothers from the age of five and for more than four decades he remained a fixture on the American entertainment scene. The interesting thing about Michael, unlike many young singers of the present generation, his lyrics were plain, simple, fun-filled and harmless. Whether as a member of the Jackson 5, a band his father Joe organized as a former musician, or as a solo act, Mr. Jackson was a prolifically creative songwriter who seemed to own the pop charts. As such, he is the only pop star inducted into music's Hall of Fame twice, as a member of the Jackson 5 and as a solo act.

Michael Jackson first appeared in Harlem at the Apollo Theather's Amateur Night at the age of 5, with his brothers and stole the show. Then known as the Jackson Brothers, in 1968, the group was signed by Berry Gordy's Motown Records. Diana Ross probably made the introductions. However, within no time, Michael and the group was a sensation. Brooks Barnes (June 26, 2009: 22) notes: "The Jackson 5 was an instant phenomenon. The group's first four singles – "I want you back," "ABC," "The Love You Save," and "I'll Be There" – all reached No. 1 on the pop charts in 1970, a feat no other group had accomplished before. And young Michael was the center of attention: he handled virtually all the lead vocals, danced with energy and finesse, and displayed a showmanship rare in a performer of any age."

The next year he began a solo career and a year after that in 1972 he produced "Ben" title song of the movie about a young kid and his pet rat considered a killer animal. While still composing, singing and dancing, Michael Jackson made his movie debut in The Wiz in 1978 alongside Diana Ross and Nipsey Russell.

"Off the Wall Sonnets" for Michael Jackson Photo.

"OFF THE WALL SONNETS" FOR MICHAEL JACKSON

"Off the Wall Sonnets" for Michael Jackson Photo. "A voice worth millions that rings through the ages!"

"I don't understand racism. We are all the same and I have the perfect hypothesis to prove it." **Michael Jackson**

15. MICHAEL JACKSON POSTSCRIPT

As the shocking details of Michael Jackson's purported drug use and addiction surfaced after his death, TV stations and other media were having field-days feeding at the trough of the pop star's misfortune. I seem to remember having a conversation with someone about a mutual friend who was inflicted with the AIDS virus. He was quick to point out, the fellow had an illness, and we needed to be compassionate about his illness. The same can hold true for Michael Jackson who equally suffered from an illness, which is the malady of addiction to prescription drugs.

As a successful person, challenged by the rigors of his profession and the demands to consistently produce at an optimum level, in this case, producing award winning hit songs, the physical demands on the entertainer, probably accidental misfortunes, his skin condition and plastic surgeries, all started him on the road to using prescription drugs. Perhaps the hurt from the child molestation allegations and the disappointment of "betrayal by important people in Hollywood" have also been instrumental in the pain Michael endured. We should never forget, Leonard Rowe, one time friend and concert promoter, in that interview along with Joe Jackson on Larry King Live, confessed when he first met Michael some thirty years ago, let's say around 1978, Michael was afraid to drink a soda! How then did he transform into the addicted monster the media gorges on in satiation as they sensationalize the latter developments in his life.

Not being sympathetic, showing empathy or commiseration at the pop star's descent into the hellishness of prescription drug addiction and the toll it has taken as he tried to manifest a semblance of normalcy, move in and out of recluse; yet feed the demands of a fan base constantly wanting more from their idol, is a demanding experience few could imagine. The media was very insensitive in this respect.

The tragedy of Michael Jackson's later lifelong road of pain, suffering and ultimately ruin, can essentially be attributable to three sets of circumstances, each playing itself out singularly, yet interacting.

First, we must list the demands associated with entertainment performance excellence such as long hours spent in perfection of his explosive and exerting dance routines; the creative exertion that earned him superstardom, as an entertainer like no other; his mishap in the Pepsi Commercial; and the numerous plastic surgeries he underwent to transform his physical appearance. Whether this latter self-mutilation is dissatisfaction with his appearance as a black man, as some have perhaps, wrongfully argued; or, the necessary sacrifices to accomplish the universal a-raciality some believe he sought to accomplish, we'll never know. However, the price of success in whatever venture is oftentimes arduous and many times painful, extremely painful. The result is he ended up dead. To this we can add the rigorous financial and other challenges to him and family as well as the embarrassment of the ordeals of accusations of child molestation; accused, charged, but never anything conclusively proven!

As in any major "coup" or accomplishment, seldom can anyone claim "I did it alone." The general-consensus is there's more "We" than "I." Sure, Frank Sinatra claimed "I did it my way," but the belief is that he was helped. Equally, Bernie Madoff, wants the public to believe he single-handedly orchestrated a $50 billion Ponzi scheme over a great many years, unknown and unaided by others. Michael Jackson, on the other hand, was surrounded by an enormous entourage of enablers, in addition to producers, writers, directors, agents, lawyers, doctors, friends, managers, the list is endless of people coming and going out of his life. A recent probe indicates he used 19 aliases to obtain prescription drugs as his addiction worsened. There were plastic surgeons, dermatologists, medical nurses, personal servants and employees. Are we to believe no one knew what was going on? No one had the "marbles" to say, "Wait a minute Kid, you're on the precipice of the cliff." Well, he fell over! Meanwhile, the media has not been kind to Michael Jackson. In 2002, he complained at Al Sharpton's National Action Network forum on racism in the music industry that, after he broke music record sales, he was villainized, the media being a useful and willing tool. This has not stopped up until his death and beyond. Let's face it, sensationalism about Michael Jackson sells papers and attracts viewers on TV programs.

After his death, local papers featured headlines among others that truthfully read "The Vultures are Circling" and "Wolves at the Door." Now the vultures have landed, and wolves are in the door! As the Coroner stalled in releasing the results of the autopsy and the realization Michael was addicted to prescription painkillers, viewers were especially glued to their

TVs to be apprised of the next piece of juicy scandal. As the "exception proves the rule," Jim Moret and other TV personalities appeared on CNN, to report on Michael or to replace Larry King, certainly other networks and newspapers followed suit. Jim Moret as the "clean cut" reporter type delved into Michael Jackson and the caption showed he covered Michael's child molestation trial. He also covered O.J. Simpson's trial for CNN. He was part of the dynamic fanaticism manifested at "Camp OJ" along with Greta Van Susteren, Dominic Dunn for *Vanity Fair* and Jeffrey Tubin of CNN who were among those who "indulged" with the sensationalism created around this black man on the ropes, incidentally also found not guilty of murder. Such "feeding" probably began with Bryon Styron's Nat Turner's execution, Marcus Garvey's trial and imprisonment, the hounding of Paul Robeson, Mohammed Ali, Mike Tyson, etc. Nevertheless, many modern analysts, commentators, reporters, from unfortunate circumstances jump started lucrative careers that are today respected in their fields.

"Off the Wall Sonnets" for Michael Jackson Photo. Redd Foxx, "The funniest man in show comedy business.

Two months after his death, before his burial events focus on doctors who administered to Michael, perhaps their actions contributed to his death. Claims of child molestation and sexual abuse have subsided, gone away, which question their originality. The media focused on Michael's words criticizing his father Joe on *Oprah*; but disregarded his own words he was innocent of child molestation, **that he was hounded because he broke all records in the music industry and for ultimately possessing the Beatles' song catalogue**. Jermaine confessed on Larry King Live that Joe was a good father, he was strict and that such were child raising methods of his generation. He held a positive view of their father pointing to the successes of the Jackson children raised by Joe Jackson.

"Off the Wall Sonnets" for Michael Jackson Photo.

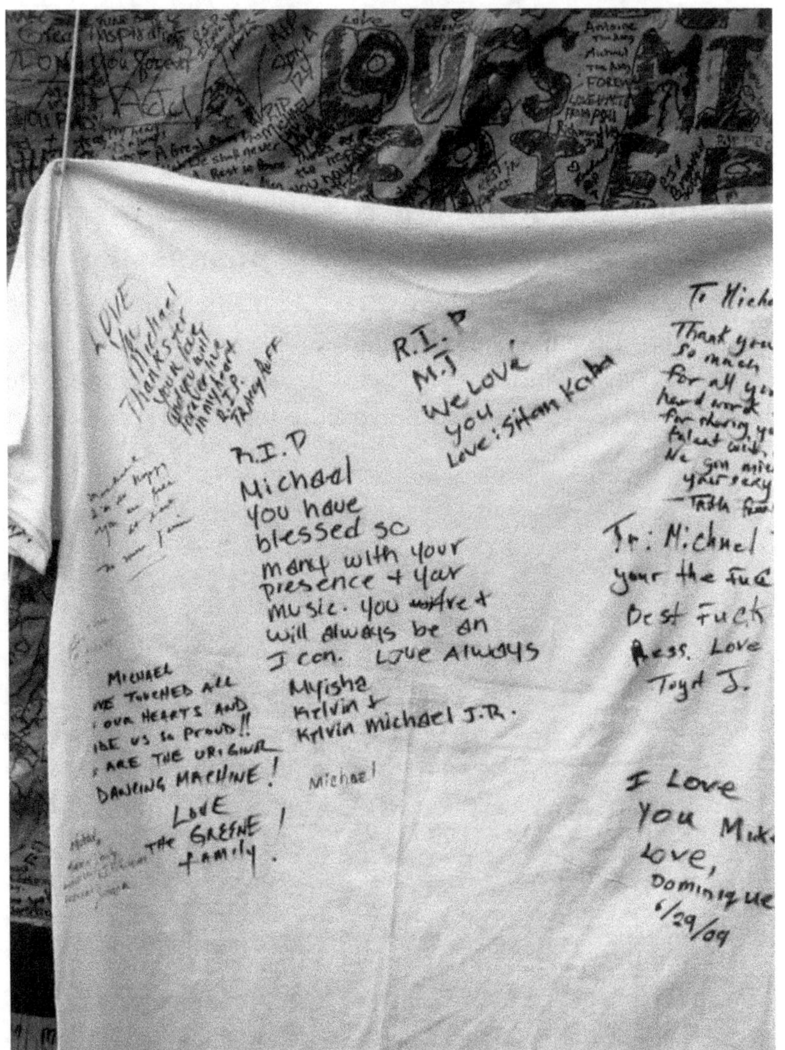

"Off the Wall Sonnets" for Michael Jackson Photo. The message is clear.

In the case of Jim Moret, representing Larry King recently, as he focused on Michael's drug addiction and enablers in the process, he seemed to lose sight of the sensational young singer Nisha who told him: "Michael was the nicest human being I met in my life." When asked, "What was the nicest thing he ever said to you," she responded: "If you take an average singer and give them a wonderful song, they will do well. If you take an amazing singer and give them a wonderful song, they will do amazingly well." This truthful and heartfelt assessment rocketed her youthful confidence and career. Such is a fitting epithet for Michael Jackson, whose unfortunate ending, capping an extraordinary career, was entrapped in the frailties of human realities, destructiveness and the powerlessness of excess. If only the media had been less sensational, more kind and compassionate, who knows when Michael got to the fork in the road, he may have turned right rather than left. Notwithstanding, he has left his mark, his legacy, his foundation, his trust, his charities, his earning power, and though now dead, he still makes the news.

Some commentators have argued since science is so highly developed in its focus on the brain, the Coroner's removing a piece of Michael's brain to test for drug substance was really an attempt to seek to understand his outstanding genius. They can do that you know!

What a remarkable individual he was who has indelibly imprinted musically upon his generation and generations to come because he expended great energy crafting his creative abilities to rise to the very top in so many categories of human artistic endeavor.

"Off the Wall Sonnets" for Michael Jackson Photo.

"Off the Wall Sonnets" for Michael Jackson Photo. "Love is the Message, MJ!"

"OFF THE WALL SONNETS" FOR MICHAEL JACKSON

Further, some have argued, it seems the media is so obsessed with reporting bad news, it could not report a positive story. It could not, even if, as E.F. Hutton used to say, "It would sneak up, slap you on the bottom and say, I'm here." The "clean cut" types would not give legs to a story saying Michael Jackson entered a Jacuzzi with a friend suffering from AIDS to show brotherly love; or that, two warring factions insisted "Let's suspend fighting, Michael Jackson is passing through," and afterwards returned to their previous belligerence; or his asking the need and then getting up to secure a glass of water for State Senator, now Governor, David Patterson, of New York.

Finally, let's not forget Paris' final and emotionally charged plea at the Memorial expressing the general-consensus "Michael Jackson was a great father." He was also a good friend, an insistently well read and creative artist; a wonderful humanitarian and in his social relations a compassionate and caring individual who should be remembered for the many positive things he did rather than the few frailties he was accused of as a human being.

This brings us back to the intent of the Apollo Memorial and the foresightful-ness of Rev. Al Sharpton. Instantly upon Michael's death Sharpton called for the Apollo Tribute because he had been a friend of Michael Jackson and Michael was a True Apollo Legend. Equally important, as himself a victim of Media vilification, familiar with the wrongs done Michael by orchestrated media, Al Sharpton rightfully got out, ahead of the curve, to steer the perception and help shape and preserve the true legacy of Michael Joseph Jackson. He was a singer, songwriter, dancer, entertainer, humanitarian, child professing love to creatively heal the world to make it a better place for you and me. Now with Jordan Chandler's purported "Internet Confession" that his father, Evan Chandler, made him lie about the child molestation charges, one has to wonder about the nature of people and why the media never, to this day, relentlessly got to and ferreted out the truth that would have aided rehabilitation of Michael's name, image and psychological we-being. Still, in the final analysis, it is the extraordinary creativity expressed in his body of work that will define how Michael Jackson is remembered for decades to come, and not the trumped-up charges so many believe were false.

"Off the Wall Sonnets" for Michael Jackson Photo. "A funny man, perhaps only second to Redd Foxx!"

"Off the Wall Sonnets" for Michael Jackson Photo. To all the Pretty Young Things" Michael appealed to, Crystal echoes the sentiments for them all.

"OFF THE WALL SONNETS" FOR MICHAEL JACKSON

"I'm really-very self-confident when it comes to my work. When I take on a project, I believe in it 100%. I really put my soul into it. I'd die for it. That's how I am." **Michael Jackson**

16. POST - POST-SCRIPT

It seems the whole story about Michael Jackson may never be fully known and in light of the media's current emphasis on his addiction and prescription drug use, it's wonderful to have any form of good news.

On Tuesday, August 4, 2009, Larry King interviewed Frank Dileo, former and then re-hired manager of Michael Jackson. Frank, expressing great empathy and sadness at the loss of his friend, indicated he managed Michael from 1984 to 1989, and again was rehired in March 2009, to be part of his entourage in the upcoming "This Is It" tour sponsored by AEG.

First, Frank said he got a call there was an ambulance at Michael's residence and when he arrived at the hospital, a nurse informed him Michacl "would not make it." Then he called "Katherine first" to explain the situation. Then he "called Joe Jackson who was already informed by others. With a doctor and social worker" he "informed the children their father had passed away."

Frank Dileo pointed out Michael Jackson was "a kind soul, who would not harm a child." Larry King mentioned his interview with Joe Jackson and Leonard Rowe and brought up the number of shows, remarking Leonard said Michael only agreed to 10 shows. Frank said no. Both he and Michael read the contract and that Michael wanted to best Prince's 21 concerts. He wanted the **Guinness Book of World Record** officials to witness his record 50 shows, because "Michael is a very competitive person." He talked about a minimum and maximum number of shows and that "there was ticket potential for 85 shows."

Jim Moret then joined the group and said: "Frank, Brooke Shields and Paris revealed a different side of Michael." He did add, however, Michael was odd.

Frank responded, "Sometimes odd can be confused. I learned a few things off Michael Jackson. Michael knew how to sell tickets." Then Larry King asked about child abuse accusations. Frank responded: "Michael was a kind soul, who won't harm a soul. The people are moochers. I told Michael to fight the first accusation. I knew he was innocent." Surprisingly, Larry King offered, "Well that seems to be going away now." This fell flat. No one responded, especially Jim Moret, to an accusation fueled by media sensationalism that persecuted a good man, damaged his image and imagination and threatened to stain his legacy. In retrospect the Al Sharpton's immediate insistence after Michael's death, the need for the Apollo Memorial and the desire to protect his legacy from false accusations, was a stroke of brilliance, "beating back wolves at the door."

Again, Larry brought up Leonard Rowe and the last meeting. Frank admitted he was not there at the Beverly Hills Hotel and Bungalow but that Michael, Joe, Leonard and Randy Phillips were there. He added Leonard did receive "The Letter" from Michael severing their relationship. Michael told him after the meeting, "Frank we have to remove Leonard." No one commented on Joe Jackson's earlier claim he was "Shouting with Randy Phillips." Frank closed by saying "allegations about Michael and children are not true." He said further, "Michael did not like family interfering in his business."

How strange, this was a manager Michael fired or severed in 1989 and again rehired in March of 2009. We are to believe everything he said, including Michael's statement regarding Leonard Rowe. However, we need not believe anything Rowe said, question Joe's intent and disregard or not pay much attention to the manager's claim that Michael was innocent of child molestation! Larry did not ask Frank if Michael explained why Joe was shouting at Randy!

Now, in view of this fellow Jordan Chandler's purported confession that his father, Evan chandler, insisted he frame Michael for money is an issue the media should follow relentlessly to clear the man's name they have so insisted was true and made so much money and ratings. This story has grown tremendously since it was first published on the Internet. It has been mainly carried by blogs. One report claims it was a hoax. Another pointed out: "No major news media source has been able to substantiate this claim."

The Urban Politico, an Internet source, of July 5, 2009, under the heading "All I want to say is they don't really care about us" has written:

"Sometime after Michael's passing last week is when the rumors started to buzz around the Internet that, if true, would confirm what many of us believed to be true 16 years ago: Michael Jackson didn't do it."

"I don't know if Jordan Chandler truly made this admission or whether it's just the internet rumor-mill hard at work, but what I do know is that the facts on the Chandler side of the story have never seemed to add up. If the boy really was molested, then it is difficult to imagine why the family of the "victim" was not at all concerned with pressing charges when it had the chance to do so after the financial settlement. So after the multi-million-dollar settlement was reached, I suppose the family figured justice had been served?"

"In sum, I'll reiterate that I am unable to verify if the alleged admission by Jordan Chandler actually-took place. But if it did, that must have been an awful lot of guilt resting on that man's heart for the past 16 years."

Nevertheless, the important thing about the book **Michael! The Apollo Memorial**, a classic collector's item, from which much of is that all along the focus has been on showing Michael Jackson in a constructively positive, humanitarian manner, as a tremendously creative artist and never accepting any false claims against "Michael, the Archangel." Whether or not the Chandler supposed confession is true, only God knows since many have tried to substantiate the claim. Notwithstanding, Michael cannot be hurt by this allegation anymore, but maybe, and if the "confession" is true, then the young man will have to face himself and his conscience for many years to come.

"Off the Wall Sonnets" for Michael Jackson Photo.

"OFF THE WALL SONNETS" FOR MICHAEL JACKSON

"Off the Wall Sonnets" for Michael Jackson Photo.

"Off the Wall Sonnets" for Michael Jackson Photo.

"Off the Wall Sonnets" for Michael Jackson Photo. So many people, so much love for such a gentle soul.

"I play to all those countries, and they cry in all the same places in my show. They laugh in the same places. They become hysterical in the same places. They faint in the same places and that's the perfect hypothesis. There is a commonality that we are all the same." Michael Jackson

17. MICHAEL JACKSON: THE FINAL WORD

Michael Jackson was indeed a very special breed of humanity, one who comes along perhaps once in a century. When you combine the many talents he possessed, his work ethic, care and concern for humanity and charitable mindset, we have the essentials of a really good person. When you combine these attributes, if his efforts to please, pleasure, protect and plead, protest and take significant steps to protect the wonderful nature of humanity and the world we live in, by some religious standards, he would have approached "sainthood." However, while personally religious, he lived a life that globally brought much joy and pleasurable moments that soothed the hearts and feelings of many people for many years. So much so, his passing was a great loss to humanity since he so gracefully and unselfishly sought to help and heal in whatever manner he could.

"Off the Wall Sonnets" for Michael Jackson Photo. The tribute is self-evident.

While many may offer thoughts garnered from their associations with Michael Jackson, whether for personal gain or not, they should really channel their aim to rehabilitate a wonderful soul, painfully exploited in his lifetime. That is, their efforts ought to be directed at "solving the mystery" of accusations that have tarnished the career and persona of an extraordinarily gentle soul. Yet still, and oftentimes, in the hustle and bustle, we seldom get a glimpse of the "inner workings" of such a gifted yet un-pretentious person. One such occasion occurred, and for those who may be fans yet never enjoyed a "close-up" with Michael, the famous Oprah interview provided such a glimpse. This certainly does not emphasize the bashing of his father for Michael rehabilitated Joe at Oxford University

Conducting her interview as any host would, Oprah ventured into a personal side of Michael. Framed in a manner, she first asked whether he was dating Brooke Shields and received an affirmative nod. Next, in a loaded question she insisted people wanted to know whether Michael was a "virgin." After all, she stated essentially, "You sing of wanting to 'Rock with you all night.' "We want to know who you rocking with!"

"Off the Wall Sonnets" for Michael Jackson Photo. Stevie Wonder, "The Blind Genius," could "see creativity, inspiration and humanity in Michael Jackson!"

But, Michael, in that gently soft voice and unpretentious manner responded seemingly as no one else would. He told Oprah, "I am a gentleman and would never discuss that." How gentlemanly of him, for so many others would want to project their macho nature, boasting and if not telling all, certainly coming close to leave the audience on the cusp to draw conclusions that seem pointedly self-evident.

That is the Michael so many imagined but seldom get to know. Importantly, from that simple response one could easily dismiss the allegations the media straddled him with for so many years. Out of respect, as with any historical figure, they should further investigate and clear his name so Michael could be properly rehabilitated and take his proper place among those who preached and practiced the good for all humanity.

"Off the Wall Sonnets" for Michael Jackson Photo. Now, here's a family, perhaps more than one generation that enjoyed the creative genius at work.

"Off the Wall Sonnets" for Michael Jackson Photo.

"Off the Wall Sonnets" for Michael Jackson Photo. Such heart-felt sentiments expressed for an Icon.

"I do believe deeply in perfection. I'm never satisfied!" **Michael Jackson**

18. MICHAEL JACKSON: THOUGHTS ON THE FUNERAL

Michael Jackson was finally buried September 3, 2009, 70 days after his passing on June 25. Himself a legend, he will lay alongside great musical and movie legends at the historic 290-acre **Forest Lawn Cemetery in Glendale, California**. He will rest in the Hollow Terrace section of the Mausoleum bearing Michelangelo-like Sistine Chapel depictions and Da Vinci's *Last Supper*. Michael himself had commissioned his own *Last Supper* which lay above his bed at Neverland. He was buried wearing a silver glove, according to his sister Janet. We are told further, Paris placed a crown upon his gold covered casket, adorned with white flowers, in another of those wonderfully moving tributes the young lady demonstrated in appreciation of the love and affection she held for her father.

As indicated in the beautiful invitation, this was a private ceremony hosted by the family with the media not permitted within the cemetery gates. Because of special considerations, the cemetery area is a no-fly zone prohibiting flyover for media coverage from the air. Yet, with powerful lens, they provided distance coverage from beyond the marker. Some 60 media outlets from around the world lined the adjacent vicinity while police kept fans and onlookers two blocks away. Still, from the air coverage CNN showed the 200-seat arrangement being filled up by arriving guests and tracked the 31-car motorcade bringing Michael's body, while CNN reporter Randi Kaye, from outside the front gate identified as many celebrities as possible as they alighted from their cars. Among celebrities identified as being in attendance Elizabeth Taylor who had stayed away, came out. So too did Quincy Jones, despite his not wanting to "attend any more funerals." Michael's friend Macaulay Caulking, Corey Feldman, Chris Tucker, Mila Kunis, and Barry Bonds, were among so many others who paid final respects to the musical genius.

"Off the Wall Sonnets" for Michael Jackson Photo.

"Off the Wall Sonnets" for Michael Jackson Photo. This is a serious message, a serious request!

Slated to begin at 10:00 pm EST (7:00 PST) the funeral ceremony was late getting started. The family released their own regulated video portions of events on a delayed basis, which the networks aired in split screen coverage. Meanwhile Larry King Live hosted individuals who offered commentary before departing to be part of the ceremony laying Michael in his final place of rest. Others as Deepak Chopra and his son Gotham Chopra remained to provide commentary and recount their experiences with the fallen star.

It is interesting that at a private funeral such as this only select people were invited. Among those invited was Leonard Rowe who had appeared on Larry King and left to attend the funeral. When we consider what was said about Leonard Rowe, especially by Frank Dileo that Michael wanted him out of the picture, if so; the question becomes 'Why would Leonard be invited to the private funeral?' It is not clear if Frank was invited. Many others who expressed all kinds of wild thoughts about Michael, and since the guest list was not made public, we don't know if they were invited.

"OFF THE WALL SONNETS" FOR MICHAEL JACKSON

We were told by Janet Jackson, among the memorabilia Michael was buried with, his black Fedora and sequined glove were included as tools of his trade, that he probably wore as he "Moon walked" through Heaven's door on his way to become a member of the heavenly choir!

"Off the Wall Sonnets" for Michael Jackson Photo. The Temptations, a put together combination of talent, creativity and style.

"Off the Wall Sonnets" for Michael Jackson Photo.

"Children are loving, they don't gossip, they don't complain, they're just open-hearted. They're ready for you. They don't judge. They don't see things by way of color." **Michael Jackson**

19. A FINAL TAKE – Was Michael Jackson a role model for young black males? By Dr. Fred Monderson

Recently a gentleman posed the question 'Was Michael Jackson a role model for young black males?' and then he came again asking 'What do you think his impact has been on these young men?' I responded, "You said impact and that is it!" Naturally he was not satisfied with such an answer, so I had to explain further.

Michael Jackson impacted soulfully not just black males but across the cultural, racial, gender and age spectrums, from celebration of birthdays, christening, graduation, bus ride, cookout, party, hangout, night of sweet serenade, boat ride, dance hall, perhaps even at Bar Mitzvahs, and even rum shops, bar and night spot entertainment. Still, these occasions and venues do not bridge the chasm of the great man's impact.

Michael Jackson gave unprecedented access to the Black Press, viz., Ebony, Jet, Essence, etc., at a time when they were coming into their own and their constituency was satiated with negative or irrelevant news. Meanwhile the band played on as Michael continued to sing, dance and entertain blunting the challenges to black males and females in an America slowly emerging from its unimagined past confronted by the Civil Rights Movement.

"OFF THE WALL SONNETS" FOR MICHAEL JACKSON

Many have confessed, particularly from Gary Indiana, they felt a sense of great joy and pride when they could sit and watch TV enjoying a young black boy and his brothers command the stage as entertainers. Michael's lyrical creativity opened doors and probably motivated young people to be song writers and ultimately make headway in the music industry. While there was much anger in America, Michael presented, manifested and represented nothing but joy, brotherhood and love for humanity.

As a consummate performer Michael gave his all, never holding back. I'm reminded of a quote of Leonard Rowe in volume I, Michael Jackson: The Apollo Memorial in which he stated: "I told Michael he has to slow down with all that dancing and he responded, I can't do that, I have to give my fans all of me." As such, Michael set the bar high, certainly indicating to young black males, whatever you do, do it to the best of your ability.

Many people get hung up on changes in Michael's physical anatomy and this is their biggest criticism of him, seeming to indicate he was ashamed of his blackness. To recall, at Al Sharpton's Forum on Racism in the Musical Industry, Michael stated clearly, "I know I'm black!" Michael Jackson was a shrewd showman who knew how to sell tickets! Let's face it. Al Jolson painted his face. Bozo the clown was an entertainer who dressed by putting on his oversized shows, baggy pants, red nose, simulated bald head, etc., and went out to perform as part of a show. Then he changed and went about his business. Michael Jackson was the show! He sculptured his appearance to permanently reflect this entertainer status, then he went out and gave them the business. It's like Frank Dileo said, "Michael knew how to sell tickets!" Michael's most loyal fans could care less what he did to his face, all they wanted was to enjoy his music, which they have done, whether he was here or gone to augment that great orchestra in the sky. Michael didn't drop his pants, he raised it up!

An even more meaningful example Michael set for black males is recounted to challenge a recent survey that concluded, 'When black males die, they do not leave anything for their offsprings.' Michael died leaving millions for his family and that is certainly a good role model example for all people.

Michael Jackson was a tremendous humanitarian, philanthropist who cared for the sick, orphaned and less fortunate. He visited hospitals, orphanages and donated untold millions to charities. In my book, anyone who takes time to visit the hospitals and orphanages to show concern for the sick and less or fortunate as well as putting his money where his mouth is, is certainly above reproach. More people should be doing that instead of spilling ink in spurious and scurrilous endeavors. For his philanthropic work, Michael Jackson was a man among men. Any young black male who seeks a role model must examine the whole picture of the man, and they would find, 'pound for pound' Michael Jackson, whether for his work ethic, his generosity, espousing love for humanity or just plain artistic skill and creative spirit, has and will always be 'a cut above.'

"Off the Wall Sonnets" for Michael Jackson Photo.

"OFF THE WALL SONNETS" FOR MICHAEL JACKSON

"Off the Wall Sonnets" for Michael Jackson Photo. "Michael can see all the love we are displaying!"

20. THE LEGACY OF MICHAEL JACKSON

By Dr. Fred Monderson

History has always shown "Good triumphs over evil" and the goodness Michael Jackson exhibited over more than four decades as an entertainer, humanitarian, philanthropist and businessman, and father, son, inventor and human being in general manner so pleasing to the almighty, is what posterity will remember of a man, many times victimized in unproven allegations.

At the Apollo Tribute, Tuesday, June 30, 2009, Rev. Al Sharpton commanded the audience to "tell our stories and to talk about Michael's legacy. He was not a freak, he was an innovator ... he was an extraordinary entertainer and we love him with extraordinary love." Herb Boyd in the *Amsterdam News* (July 2 - July 8, 2009) informed how "love for Michael is universal, and there is no better testament to his power and influence as an artist and entertainer than the millions around the globe who were shocked by his sudden death as they were awed by his incomparable talent."

Checked early, the work of the wolves, vultures, vampires and zombies who fed at his lucrative trough will be forgotten in time. Along with their architects, they will either be consigned to footnotes in history or overshadowed by the sheer bulk of the positive contribution of a mega star of towering fame, not unlike a comet, that only passes this way "once in a very long time."

First, Michael Jackson will be remembered for his enormous body of work, particularly the earliest and freshest of his productions that exhibited great magnitude, vision, simplicity and charged fun-filled emotions. His lyrics, style and grace appealed to many people across race, culture and religion where parents, white, black, brown and yellow, felt comfortable with their children listening to and imitating young black boys in their living rooms. The Jackson 5 recorded 14 albums with Motown Records, and Michael also did 4 solo albums with the company. Yet, these early creations simply set the stage for the maturing genius of an emerging solo artist with extraordinary talent, who, in teaming up with music impresario Quincy Jones, produced even more mega hits following his departure from Motown.

One commentator wrote, in "Don't Stop" ('Til you get enough) - the music riveted attention: Jackson' imperial achievement 'Thriller.' The first single 'Billie Jean' began with a uniquely undulating bass line that Jackson topped with a frenzy of curt breaths and huffy exhales. The interplay between Jackson' Jim Farber's "A Wacko yes, but also a genius in many ways," in *Daily News* Friday, June 26, 2009, p. 4, referred to Michael and Quincy's "Off the Wall" production as, "a work that gave their mix of funk, soul, jazz and pop a universal stamp. From the opening track - (Don't Stop) His falsetto had both vulnerability and confidence and the music ruled the dance floor." Then he writes about "Jackson's inventive vocals and the forceful music entranced pop fans in every country around the world."

His creative genius, coupled with energetic performances full of life and exhibiting incomparable dance moves enabled "Off The Wall" and "Thriller" and their videos to break down the segregated walls of MTV and, importantly, aiding the music station's solvency. It also opened the door for African American performers to be aired on MTV's popular cable TV network. Michael won 8 Grammys for "Thriller," the most by a single artist. The album boasted 7 No. 1 hit singles. It sold more than 100 million copies worldwide. After its 1982 release, it stayed 37 weeks on the charts as No. 1. "Off the

Wall" had sold more than 20 million albums worldwide after its 1979 release. Michael's efforts revitalized economic aspects of the music industry in devastating musical brilliance.

Year after year, Michael Jackson wrote and produced award winning music that sold millions of records and he continued to fill venues when on tour and in concerts. Excitement and anticipation awaited his every performance and this was no doubt the case with his last scheduled set of appearances. Randy Tarraborelli, who wrote a biography about Michael Jackson informed: "The primary reason for the concerts wasn't so much that he wanted to generate money, as much as it was that he wanted to perform for the kids. They had never seen him perform before."

Nayaba Arinde (July 2-July 8, 2009) described him as a "man who changed the music game with his singing; dancing; writing and producing." Michael also vocally protested racism in the music industry. Michael Jackson had a down-to-earth quality about him. In June 2002, Michael asked the **National Action Network** audience "What's more important than giving people a sense of escapism?" "What would life be without a song, joy, laughter and music?"

Selling more than 750 million albums, plus untold numbers of singles, of which 13 were No. 1 as a solo artist, the winning of 13 Grammy Awards, 8 for "Thriller" and awarded 2, a never before and since accomplished, introductions into the Rock and Roll Hall of fame; one as a member of the Jackson 5 and one as a solo artist, Michael has had a very distinguished creative career. These distinctions established Michael Jackson as an unparalleled and extraordinary entertainer possessing talent seemingly inspired by divine guidance. Again, Michael's soft spoken nature seemed spiritually and mystically divine and his humanitarian nature underscored that godly connection destined to do good for those in need.

"OFF THE WALL SONNETS" FOR MICHAEL JACKSON

As an interesting article by Edna Gunderson in **USA Today** (July 2, 2009) entitled "The King of Pop reigns over Music Charts," graphically chronicles initial purchasing reactions to the passing of Michael Jackson, because of his melodious sweet harmonic and joyful expression in his songs and videos; their sales are sure to set trends for generations and generations of love and respect for the man and his music.

His message was clear, just like Michael! Even more important, and this should be a reminder to all, while Michael Jackson' legacy is assured it is also not tarnished, thanks to the efforts of Rev. Al Sharpton and others who would not let the media wolves devour the lifeless body and image of "our golden boy." Sharpton's message at the Apollo Memorial was unequivocal: "We love and will defend our heroes." That is, from the destructive machinations of the vultures, vampires and unsavory characters who not only sully people's character and image, but grow rich in the process.

Even more significant, Michael's legacy is also evident in his good works, his humanitarianism, and his charitable work through contributions and physically visiting the "trenches of maladies." Michael has been praised, beyond his creative and artistic genius, as being a "take no prisoners showman and entertainer;" but also as a shrewd businessman and one who shared his bread. He was also a master at give back! This generosity certainly went a long way in "netting" his enemies' "swoop down" in his most vulnerable moments!

Because of the symbolism of Michael Jackson and the Jackson 5 in the early years of their careers; in aftermath of the Civil Rights Movement, Black newspapers particularly **Ebony**, **Esquire**, **Jet**, and many others including **Peoples Weekly**, **Time**, **TV Guide**, **Glamour**, **Ladies Home Journal**, **Life**, **Newsweek**, **Vogue**, **Publishers Weekly**, and other magazines, radio and early TV programs carried the image, spread the word and this helped raise people's consciousness to their goodness, creativity and otherwise. This local exposure helped stamp his enormous imprint on black and white culture. Such groundswell response is what encouraged Michael Jackson to begin his low-key give back that later mushroomed into Guinness Book of World Records recognition of his charitable giving. Michael underwrote projects, he visited the sick, and he fed the poor, all this at home and abroad. He "helped cancer-stricken children, burn victims, terminally ill children, -and those with illnesses as AIDS and juvenile diabetes." He worked for social justice! He visited and assisted the less fortunate in Africa and when he finally realized the gravity of poverty in Africa, he formed the Heal the World Foundation. Then he produced, wrote and performed, with Lionel Richie, "We Are the World" and "Heal the World" and played his part in "Live Aid."

In as much as one's legacy is also shaped by what that individual leaves behind and since Michael Jackson left much of his work, the revenues gained there from will continue to support his charitable works. Michael's mother, Katherine, and family members of like mind including his children, will most definitely seek to see his charitable gift-giving continue. Possibly, they will support other ventures in his name; so, decades later, when a poor person wherever, at some auspicious or inauspicious occasion benefits from a meal, a coat, footwear, school supplies, a clinic, etc., they will always remember to say **GOD BLESS MICHAEL JACKSON** because he deserved it.

Whenever **THE WIZ** is performed, his version will be remembered!

"OFF THE WALL SONNETS" FOR MICHAEL JACKSON

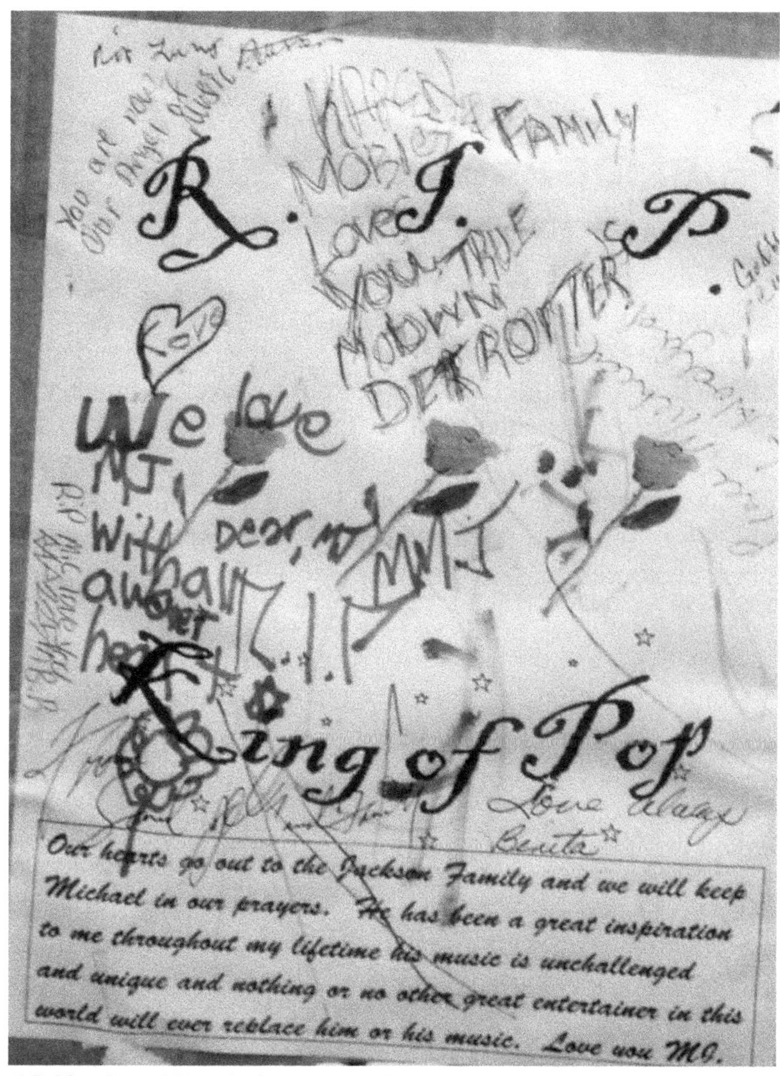

"Off the Wall Sonnets" for Michael Jackson Photo.

"Heal the world, make it a better for you and for me and the entire human race." **Michael Jackson**

21. PERIODICAL BIBLIOGRAPHICAL REFERENCE FOR FURTHER RESEARCH

The original intent of this section was to provide a database (partial) for researchers to be able to look into the life and work of Michael Jackson. That still holds. However, a number of observations have shed light on the complexity of the man, artist, musician, humanitarian, etc. It also underscores the Media's obsession with Michael Jackson and how, that obsession distorted their perception and portrayal of the phenomenon of the "King of Pop."

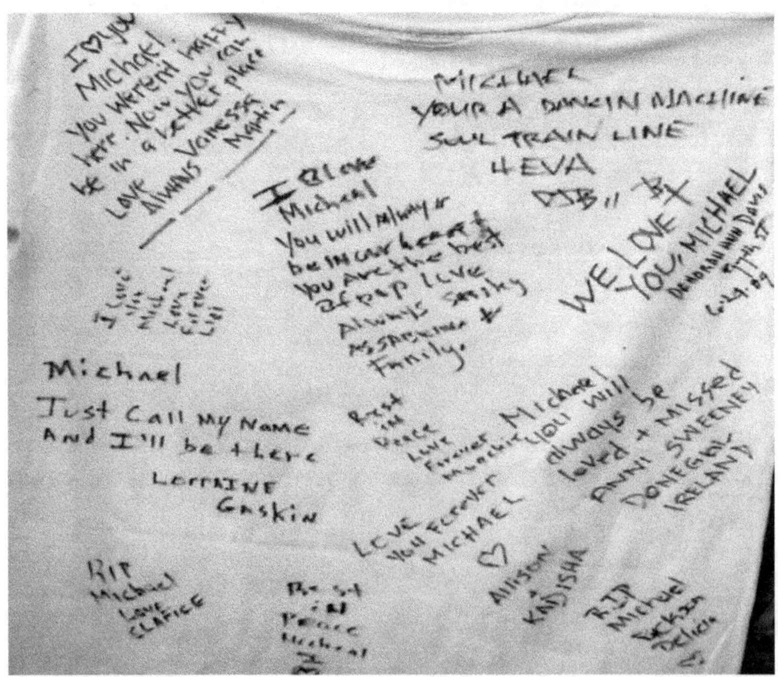

"Off the Wall Sonnets" for Michael Jackson Photo.

"OFF THE WALL SONNETS" FOR MICHAEL JACKSON

In his age, no entertainer/celebrity has had as extensive media coverage as Michael Jackson. Yet, one article seems to sum it all up: "Who's on his side?" Even more, the media has revealed contradictions in its coverage. For example, one article in *Ebony* detailed Michael Jackson's disdain for Africa on many counts. Yet he was feted even though he did not agree to perform. He was made King and enthroned. He was also made a member of a South African tribe. These developments could not have happened if he behaved in any way inappropriate with Africans when he visited that continent.

What is interesting, much of the negative press seems to have begun before Michael was accused of child molestation and that first accusation opened flood doors of the "hounding." Perhaps the signing of a contract with Sony for $600 million dollars when he did was an unimaginable development for a black man in America to be involved in. Later he had the audacity to name a small mountain on Neverland Ranch "Mount Katherine" and that too may have contributed to the animus that developed fed by the accusation. And so on and on! Well, it's all here and without a doubt Michael Jackson was an extraordinary person who brought fame not only to his person but to the people who fed off him. It is also interesting how many newspaper and magazine, even Journal covers he graced, in the feeding frenzy that followed his career.

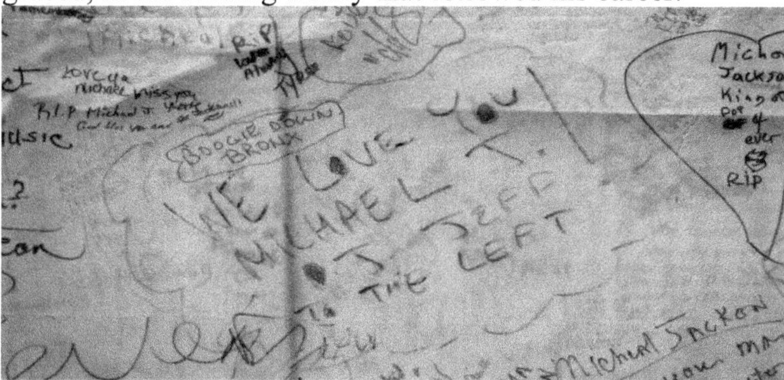

"Off the Wall Sonnets" for Michael Jackson Photo.

"Off the Wall Sonnets" for Michael Jackson Photo. An across the street view on 125th of the Celebration of Michael Jackson's passing into heavenly glory!

"Off the Wall Sonnets" for Michael Jackson Photo.

1971

"OFF THE WALL SONNETS" FOR MICHAEL JACKSON

Jackson 5 - *Life* 71: 50-51 September 24, 1971.

1977

Michael Jackson: A Young bachelor married to Music. Ill. Bob Lucas. *Jet* 52: 60-63 (March 31, 1977).

1978

Michael Jackson digs The Wiz! Interview, Ed by E. Miller. Pors. *Seventeen* 37: 270-01+ August 1978.
Blame it on the Boogie? T. White. Il. Pors. *Crawdaddy* p. 48-51 December, 1978.
Michael Jackson: Wiz kid. Por. *Teen* 23: 50+ January, 1979.
On the Move. R. Windeler. Il. Pors. *People* 10: 85-86+ November 27, 1978.

1979

Michael Jackson. Il. Robert Johnson. *Jet* 56: 30-33+ (August 16, 1979).

1980

Michael teams with Sister Latoya Jackson. Robert E. Johnson. *Jet* 15: 58-63, April 1980.
Michael Jackson: 'Wiz' Sweep Image Awards. *Jet* 15: 60-62, February 1980.

1981

Michael Jackson: Most Popular Male Entertainer. Ill. *Jet* 61: 150-52 (November 5, 1981).

1982

Michael Jackson. Ill. Charles L. Sanders. *Ebony* 38: 126-30+ November 1892.

"Off the Wall Sonnets" for Michael Jackson Photo. "Wow! MJ, You are the Light of the World!"

1983

Are Lady Di and Michael Jackson still soul mates? Il. Por. *People Weekly* 20: 28, August 8, 1983.

Diana and Michael. C.L. Sanders. Il. Pors. *Ebony* 39: 29-30+ November 1983.
Michael Jackson. G. Hirshey. Il. Pors. *Rolling Stone* pp. 120-11 + February 17, 1983.
The Peter Pan of Pop. J. Miller. Il. Pors. *Newsweek* 101: 52-4, January 10, 1983.
Thanks to a Thriller Album, the former small fry of the Jacksons become the biggest star in Pop music. Por. *People Weekly* 20: 73 December 26, 1983-January 2, 1984.

1984

All About Michael (Jackson). Il. Pors *People Weekly* 22 September issue 3-23+ November–December, 1984.
Anyone who wants a date with Michael Jackson can get 365 of them next year. Il. Por. *People Weekly* 22: 34 July 30, 1984.
The bizarre ways of Michael Jackson look-alikes. C. Krupp. Il. Por. *Glamour* 82: 61, July 1984.
Bringing back the magic. J. Cocks. Il. Por. *Time* 124: 6-65+ July 16, 1984.
A different kind of celebration. A. Haley. Por. *Ladies Home Journal* 101: 126+ December 1984.
The Glove comes off as Michael Jackson goes to work. J. McBride. Il. Por. *People's Weekly* 21: 151-2+ June 11, 1984.
It's coming, Michaelmania. Il. por. *Newsweek* 104: 26, July 2, 1984.
Jackson attempts to block Thriller film from stores. Il. Por. *Jet* 66: 16, May 28, 1984.
The Jackson Brothers grim. Por. *Esquire* 101: 88, January 1984.
The Jackson family talks about Michael. R.E. Johnson. Il. Pors. *Jet* 66: 56-60 March 26, 1984.
Jackson names Epic V.P. Frank Dileo, new manager. Disney world expands Michael Jackson Suite. Il. Por. *Jet* 66: 58-9 April 9, 1984.
Jackson Thriller gets MTV Video Music Awards. Por. *Jet* 67: 60 October 8, 1984.

Just One More Thriller. A. B. Block. Il. Por. *Forbes* 134; Spring Issue: 232 + October 1, 1984.
Making Michael Jackson Thriller. M. Cohen. Il. *High Fidelity* 34: 57-8,
The Magic of Michael Jackson. S. Weller. Il. Pors. *McCall's* 111: 38+ May 1984.
Michael! G. Smith. Il. Pors. *People's Weekly* 22: 82-4+ August 27, 1984.
Michael Jackson and Brooke Shields: they share a special friendship. Il. Pors. *Jet* 65: 14-18 February 27, 1984.
Michael Jackson didn't steal song, court rules. Il. Pors. *Jet* 67: 53-57 December 31, 1984-January 7, 1985.
Michael Jackson gives share of Victory Tour to UNCF, others. Il. Por. *Jet* 67: 56 October 15, 1984.
Michael Jackson Inc. K. Folitz. *Newsweek* 103: 66-67 February 27, 1984.
The Michael Jackson nobody knows [Interview] R. E. Johnson. Il. Pors. *Ebony* 40: 155-58 December 1984.
The Michael Jackson Syndrome. C. Rubenstein. Il. Por. *Discover* 5: 68-70, September 1984.
Michael Jackson: the world's greatest entertainer. R.E. Johnson. Il. Pors. *Ebony* 39: 163-65+ May 1984.
Michael Jackson's Money Machine. Por. *US News and World Report* 97: 14 July 16, 1984.
Michael Jackson live wire. Il. Por. Vogue 174: 450-1 March 1984.
Michael Jackson rests at home; healing of burns pleases medics. Il. Pors. *Jet* 67: 56 November 26, 1984.
Michael Jackson tells Ebony things he never talked about before; Jackson to write about his scalp operation while home. Il. Por. *Jet* 66: 55-6 May 7, 1984.
Michael weaves magic spell as he bounces back from burn bout. Il. Por. Jet 65: 54-56. February 20, 1984.
Michaelmania. Il. Por. *Ebony* 39: 120+ July 1984.
Michael's magic show. G. Hirshey. Il. Por. *Rolling Stone* p. 27-9+ August 16, 1984.
The new wizard of Opp. G. MacKay. Il. Por. *MacLean's* 97: 38-40+ July 23, 1984.

"OFF THE WALL SONNETS" FOR MICHAEL JACKSON

Singer Michael Jackson sweeps American Music Awards wins eight honors. Il. Por. Jet 65: 62 January 30, 1984.

Thriller Chiller. C. Arrington. Il. Pors. *People's Weekly* 21: 24-27 February 13, 1984.

The Tour, the Money, the Magic. J. Miller. Il. Por. *Newsweek* 104: 64-70July 16, 1984.

Why he's a Thriller. J. Cocks. Il. Pors. *Time* 123: 54-57+ March 19, 1984.

Why Michael hid out in a White House men's room and other tales of the day power played host to fame. Il. Por. *People's Weekly* 21: 75 May 28, 1984.

Bringing back the magic. J. Cocks. Il. Por. *Time* 12: 64-65 July 16, 1984.

The Jackson fireworks. W. Plummer. Il. Pors. *People's We*ekly 22: 44-47 July 23, 1984.

Jackson mania [Release of Victory]. J. Pareles. Il. *Mademoiselle* 90: 74+ November 1984.

The Jacksons dazzle New York fans; Won't bow to death threats and cancel Knoxville. Il. *Jet* 66: 54-56+ August 20, 1984.

Jacksons complete control of Victory Tour to keep million$ in family. Il. *Jet* 66: 55-56 July 9, 1984.

The Jacksons scorc an appealingly modest, almost hollow Victory. V. Aletti. Il. *Rolling Stone* p. 35+ August 16, 1984.

Jacksons hit the jackpot on U.S. Tour. M. Goldberg. *Rolling Stone* p. 56 November 8, 1984.

Mother of the Jacksons hit press lies about family, upcoming tour. Il. *Jet* 66: 54-555 June 4, 1984.

Pepsi stages two days to premiere long-awaited TV ads with the Jacksons. Il. *Jet* 66: 14-15 March 19, 1984.

1985

Can Michael Jackson keep the faith? B.G. Harrison. *Mademoiselle* 91: 142 January 1985.

Jackson pays $47.5 million for Beatles songs. D. Fricke. Il. Por. *Rolling Stone* p. 22 September 26, 1985.

Jackson pens, produces new tune for holidays. Por. *Jet* 6 8: 58 June 10, 1985.
Living With Michael Jackson. T. Gold. Il. por. *McCall's* 112: 28+ February 1985.

"Off the Wall Sonnets" for Michael Jackson Photo. "The fans are here expressing their sentiments for their Icon!"

Michael Jackson and Lionel Richie's song earns millions for Africa's famine victims. *Jet* 68: 60-64 April 8, 1985.
Michael Jackson is 'painfully' shy, says Brooke Shields on TV. Por. *Jet* 68: 61 July 15, 1985.
Michael Jackson named US teen's top hero. Il. Por. *Jet* 67: 57 January 14, 1985.
Michael Jackson pays $47.5m for Beatles hits. Il. Por. *Jet* 68: 55 September 2, 1985.
Michael Jackson undergoes airport search in London. Il. Por. *Jet* 68: 34 April 15, 1985.
Michael Testifies. M. Possley. Il. *Rolling Stones* p. 20 January, 1985.
Michael to Paul: beat it. Il. Por. *Newsweek* 106: 48 August 26, 1985.

"OFF THE WALL SONNETS" FOR MICHAEL JACKSON

Michaelmania grips London as superstar unveils his wax figure. Il. Pors. *Jet* 68: 55 April 15, 1 985.
The sound of one glove clapping. G. Hirshey. Il. *Rolling Stone* p. 11-12 December 19, 1985-January 2, 1986.

1986

25 Arts students awarded Jackson UNCF scholarships. Por. *Jet* 70: 22 April 7, 1986.
Jackson may keep giraffe at his Encino menagerie. *Jet* 70: 54 July 14, 1986.
Jackson's plans for own hyperbaric chamber nixed. Por. *Jet* 72: 38 October 20, 1986.
Michael Jackson inks a $15 million Pepsi pact. Il. Por. *Jet* 70: 56 May 26, 1986.
Michael Jackson inks multimillion-dollar deal with Pepsi. A. DeCurtis. *Rolling Stone* p. 13 June 19, 1986.
Michael Jackson may sing at Moscow's Goodwill Games. Por. *Jet* 70: 57 June 23, 1986.
Officials order Jackson to enlarge zoo for giraffe. *Jet* 70: 14 July 14, 1986.
When Disneyland debuted his 3-D movie marvel, Michael Jackson was in another dimension. S. Haller. Il. *People's Weekly* 26: 30-32 September 29, 1986.

1987

And in Ethiopia, the cult of the Gloved One. Por. *Newsweek* 109: 31 May 25, 1987.
'Bad' Michael Jackson thrills Tokyo audience during Japan tour debut. Il. Por. *Jet* 73: 4+ September 28, 1987.
The Badder they come. J. Cocks. Il. Pors. *Time* 130: 85 September 14, 1987.
For sale: the Gloved One's cast-off main squeeze. Il. Por. *People's Weekly* 27: 88 May 25, 21987.

Good news: 'Bad' news. D. Handelman. *Rolling Stone* p. 11 August 13, 1987.

Is Michael Jackson for real? [Cover story] M. Goldberg and D. Handelman. Il. Pors. *Rolling Stone* p 50-1+ September 24, 1987.

Jackson LP: early sales for 'Bad' are good. F. Goodman. *Rolling Stone* p. 15 October 8, 1987.

Michael grows up. D. Sigerson. Il. Por. *Rolling Stone* p 87-88 October 22, 1987.

Michael Jackson: Bad; Prince: Sign of the times. D. Wolff. *Nation* 245: 728-9 December 12, 1987.

Michael Jackson comes back! [Cover story] R.E. Johnson. Il. Pors. *Ebony* 42: 142-44+ September, 1987.

Michael Jackson conquers Japan and continues his world tour. [Cover story] Il. Pors. *Jet* 73: 54-57 November 9, 1987.

Michael Jackson tells Ebony about his new sole career. Il. Por. *Jet* 72: 65 September 7, 1987.

Michael Jackson to get $10 million for Pepsi ads. *Jet* 71: 22 February 9, 1987.

Michael Jackson 'Bad' album released this month. Por. *Jet* 72: 56 August 10, 1987.

Michael Jackson's newest thriller. C. McGuigan. Por. *Newsweek* 110: 69 August 3, 1987.

Michael's first epistle [cover story] M. Small. Il. Pors. *People's Weekly* 28: 102-04+ October 12, 1987.

The Peter Pan of songs and dances. V. Ross. Il. Pors. *MacLean's* 100: 57-58 September 14, 1987.

Richie talks about friend, fellow star Michael Jackson. Il. Pors. *Jet* 71: 62 February 16, 1987.

Simian star of a new toy line, Michael Jackson's pet Bubbles, plays second banana to no one. Il. *People's Weekly* 28: 189 November 16, 1987.

The trouble with Michael Jackson. J. Pareles. Il. *Mademoiselle* 93: 108+ March 1987.

Unlike anyone, even himself [cover story]. C. Durkee. Il. Pors. *People's Weekly* 28: 86-87+ September 14, 1987.

A way to play Michael. T. Jaffe. Por. *Forbes* 140: 221 September 21, 1987.

"OFF THE WALL SONNETS" FOR MICHAEL JACKSON

1988

"The 'Bad' boy and the Boss. C. McGuigan; B. Barol. Il. Pors. *Newsweek* 111: 71 March 7, 1988.

Big number. *The New Yor*ker 64: 31-32 March 14, 1988.

Bob Jones leaves Motown to handle PR for Jackson. Pors. *Jet* 73: 56 January 25, 1988.

The image culture: Michael Jackson, Cindy Sherman, and the art of self-manipulation. M. Jefferson. Il. Pors. *Vogue* 178: 122+ March, 1988.

The Invisible man returns. M. Gilmore. Il. Pors. *Rolling Stone* p. 35+ March 24, 1988.

Jackson boosting the Beatles. J. Ressner. *Rolling Stone* p. 35+ March 24, 1988.

Jackson is first to have 5 no. 1 hits on album; aids the Motown Museum. Il. Por. *Jet* 74: 54, July 25, 1988.

The man in the mirror. L. Black. Il. Por. MacLean's 101: 67 May 2, 1988.

Michael debuts his new show in Kansas City. M. Gilmore. Il. Por. *Rolling Stone* p 15+ April 7, 1988.

Michael Jackson: a new look at superstar and behind the scenes. R.E. Johnson. Il. Pors. *Jet* 73: 56-63 March 21, 1988.

Michael Jackson conquers Europe. [Cover story] Il. Pors. *Jet* 74: 62-64 August 8, 1988.

Michael Jackson donates $125,000 to Motown Museum. Il. Pors. *Jet* 75: 57-58 November 14, 1988.

Michael Jackson earns $97 million to become highest paid entertainer. Il. Por. *Jet* 75: 12 October 3, 1988.

Michael Jackson gives blacks a big piece of money action on his concert tour. Il. Pors. *Jet* 73: 52-58 March 28, 1988.

Michael Jackson plans to quit concert tours. Il. Por. *Jet* 74: 53 September 19, 1988.

Michael Jackson shares Chicago honor with his guest, Lola Falana, who is fighting MS disease. Il. Por. *Jet* 74: 54 May 9, 1988.

Michael Jackson to hit the road for limited American tour. A. De Curtis. Il. Por. *Rolling Stone* p 23 February 11, 1988.
Michael Jackson turns 30! Il. Pors. *Jet* 74: 58-59 August 29, 1988.
Michael Jackson's book reveals secrets of his success [cover story] R.E. Johnson. Il. Pors. *Jet* 74: 36-39 May 16, 1988.
Michael turns 30! Q. Troupe. Il. Pors. *Essence* 19: 52-5 4+ July 1988.
A new and revealing look at Michael Jackson [cover story] R.E. Johnson. Il. Pors. *Ebony* 43: 176+ June 1988.
On tour, he's still 'Michael!' But his charity work has won him a new title: Dr. Jackson. T. Gold. Il. Pors. *People's Weekly* 29: 36-37 March 28, 1988.
The score on Michael Jackson. T. Gold. Il. Pors. *McCall's* 115: 66-68+ August 1988.
Turning Bad into good, Motown Michael sends some concert cash back to his musical roots. J. Young. Il. Pors. *People's Weekly* 30: 143-44 November 7, 1988.
Walking softly. Il. Pors. *Newsweek* 111: 77 May 2, 1988.

1989

All bad things must come to an end as a tearful Michael Jackson bids bye-bye to the highway. S. Dougherty. Por. *People's Weekly* 31: 52-53 February 13, 1989.
Magical tours. J. Cocks. Il. Por. *Ti*me 133: 59 January 23, 1989.
Michael Jackson. R. Lacayo. Por. *People's Weekly* 32 Special Issue: 68-69 Fall 1989.
Michael Jackson and his manager Frank Dileo go their separate ways. Il. Pors. *Jet* 75: 57 March 6, 1989.
Michael Jackson earns $125 million and remains highest paid entertainer. Il. Por. *Jet* 76: 26+ October 2, 1989.
Michael Jackson gets award from his sixth-grade teacher in L.A. Il. Pors. *Jet* 77: 29 October 30, 1989.
Michael Jackson quits concert stage after world tour sets me records [cover story] R E. Johnson. Il. Pors. *Jet* 75: 54-59 February 27, 1989.

"OFF THE WALL SONNETS" FOR MICHAEL JACKSON

Michael Jackson says good-bye. M. Hammer. Il. Pors. *Ladies Home Journal* 106: 116+ May 1989.

Michael Jackson says his 18-month worldwide tour was an 'incredible journey.' Il. Por. *Jet* 75: 61 January 23, 1989.

Michael's last tour [Cover story]. Il. Por. *Ebony* 44: 142-44+ April 1989.

"Off the Wall Sonnets" for Michael Jackson Photo. One can envision the intensity of this "Pen to Paper Experience."

1990

Bush Lauds Michael Jackson as 'Entertainer of the Decade.' Il. Pors. *Jet* 78: 4-5 April 23, 1990.

Dumped by Jackson, former manager Frank Dileo bounces back as one of Hollywood's GoodFellas. T. Gold. Il. Pors. *People's Weekly* 34: 99-100 October 22, 1990.

McCartney blames Yoko for Jackson's Beatles purchase. Il. Por. *Jet* 78: 38 May 7, 1990.

Michael Jackson feted as top artist of the decade after selling 110 million discs. Il. Por. *Jet* 77: 60 March 12, 1990.

Michael Jackson opens home to 45 Dream Street Campers. Il. Por. *Jet* 78: 55 August 13, 1990.

Michael Jackson rushed to hospital suffering from chest discomfort. Por. *Jet* 78: 54 June 18, 1990.

Not yet. P. Newcomb. Il. Por. *Forbes* 146 Special Issue 8 October 33, 1990.

Portrait of Michael Jackson sells for $2.1 million. Il. Pors. *Jet* 77: 14 February 12, 1990.

1991

The biggest brother-sister stars in show business history. Il. Pors. *Ebony* 46:40 August, 1991.

Books on Jackson, Springsteen due, J. Ressner. *Rolling Stone* p. 22 February 7, 1992.

Brooke Shields rebukes critics of 'Dangerous' album by Michael Jackson. Il. Pors. *Jet* 18: 54 December 9, 1991.

A first look at Michael's "Black or white" mega-video [Cover story] S. Galloway. Il. Pors. *TV Guide* 39: 4-6 November 2-8, 1991.

The great Michael make-over. Il. Por. *People's Weekly* 35: 120-01 June 10, 1991.

Jackson, Michael: Dangerous [sound recording] Reviews

Jet – IL. Pors. 81: 58-62 December 2, 1991.

Newsweek – IL. Por., 118: 72-73 December 9, 1991. J. Leland.

Time – IL. Por. 138: 86 December 2, 1991. J. Cocks.

The Jacksons score big: Michael and Janet set new standards for artist deals. M. Goldberg. Il. Pors. *Rolling Stone* p. 15-16 May 2, 1991.

Jackson's "Thriller" glove is recovered in Detroit. Il. Por. *Jet* 81: 52 October 21, 1991.

Madonna and Michael [Cover story] S. Dougherty. Il. Pors. *People's Weekly* 35: 64-68, April 15, 1991.

Michael Jackson inks unprecedented multi-media deal with Sony. Il. Por. *Jet* 79: 56-57 April 8, 1991.

Michael Jackson to visit four African countries. Il. por. *Jet* 79: 29 January 28, 1991.

"OFF THE WALL SONNETS" FOR MICHAEL JACKSON

"Off the Wall Sonnets" for Michael Jackson Photo. Here is another example of "Fanstomania!"

1992

Bringing up Michael [Cover] s. Pond. Il. Pors. *TV Guide* 40: 8-11+ November 14-20, 1992.
Ebony/Jet interview with Michael Jackson. Por. *Ebony* 48: 126+ November 19923.
Eyewitness report on Michael Jackson's tour inside Africa [Cover story] R. E. Johnson. Il. Pors. *Jet* 81: 10-17+ March 16, 1992.
Fast start for 'Dangerous.' M. Goldberg. *Rolling Stone* 9+ January 23, 1992.
Jackson, Michael: Dangerous [sound recording] Reviews
The Nation 254: 138-39 February 3, 1992. G. Santoro
Rolling Stone IL. p. 49-51 January 9, 1992. A Light
Jackson, Michael. In the Closet [videotape] Reviews
Jet IL. Pors. 82: 56-57 April 27, 1992.
Jackson pays for burial of boy killed by random shot. Por. *Jet* 82: 6 June 8, 1992.
Jacksons ends aid supplies to children in Sarajevo. Il. Pors. *Jet* 83: 58 December 14, 1992.
Michael Jackson. Il. Por. *People's Weekly* 38: 62-63 July 27, 1992.
Michael Jackson. G. Hirshey. Por. *Rolling Stone* p. 135-36 June 11, 1992.
Michael Jackson [concert at Wembley Stadium, London] A. Light. Il. Pors. *Rolling Stone* P. 38 September 17, 1992.
Michael Jackson: Crowned in Africa, pop music king tells real story of controversial trip [cover story; with interview] R.E. Johnson. Il. Pors. *Ebony* 47: 34-36+ May 1992.
Michael Jackson kicks off dangerous tour in Europe. Il. Pors. *Jet* 82: 58 July 6, 1992.
Michael Jackson receives NABOB top achievement award. Il. Por. *Jet* 81: 57 March 30, 1992.
Michael Jackson schedules his first-ever televised concert for $20 million. Por. *Jet* 82: 58-59 August 31, 1992.
Michael Jackson signs to head Super Bowl XXVII halftime TV spectacular. Por. *Jet* 82: 22 September 28, 1992.
Michael Jackson stops fan from suicide attempt; Meets Prince of Wales. Il. por. *Jet* 82: 65 August 127, 1992.

Michael Jackson: The making of the "King of Pop" [cover story] M. Goldberg. Il. Pors. *Rolling Stone* p. 3 2-37 January 9, 1992.
Michael Jackson thrills 70,000 at historic concert in Bucharest, Romania. Il. Por. *Jet* 82: 62 October 9, 1992.
Michael Jackson wins in court; judge halts publishing of his photo by London Daily mirror. Por. *Jet* 82: 34-35 August 17, 1992.
Michael Jackson's lawyers respond to charges of copyright infringement. *Jet* 82: 60 May 11, 1992.

1993

An abuse of trust? M. Goldberg. Il. Por. *Rolling Stone* p. 21 October 14, 1993.
Choosing sides in Michael Thriller. K. Hamilton. Il. Por. *Newsweek* v 122 p. 38 December 27, 1993.
Dangerous. M. Rosen. Il. Pors. *People's Weekly* 40 p. 40-42 September 6, 1993.
Facing the music. R. Corliss. Il. Pors. *Time* 142: 67December 27, 1993.
Family and fans support Michael Jackson in child abuse investigation [cover story]. Il. Pors. *Jet* 84: 52-59 September 13, 1993.
Jackson hires black attorney Johnny Cochran to defend him against charges. Por. *Jet* 85: 61 December 20, 1993.
Jacksons' Dangerous game. A. Light. Il. *Rolling Stone* 17 April 1, 1993.
Jacksons refute Latoya's charge Michael kept boys with him at family home. Il. por. *Jet* 85: 52+ December 27, 1993-January 3, 1994.
Liz Taylor says she faced the same kind of addictions as Michael Jackson. Il. Pors. *Jet* 85: 12+ December 13, 1993.
Mega-Michael. R. Scheer. *The Nation* 257: 376-77 October 11, 1993.

Michael in Wonderland [Cover story]. D. Friend. Il. Pors. *Life* 16 52-58+ June 1993.

Michael is back, but is he bad? D. Brandy. Il. Por. *Maclean's* 106: 62 December 27, 1993.

Michael Jackson. Il. Por. *People's Weekly* 40: 48-49 December 27, 1993.

Michael Jackson and Little Richard awarded special Grammy honors. Il. Por. *Jet* 83: 52 March 15, 1993.

Michael Jackson ends world tour, blames addiction to painkillers. Il. Pors. *Jet* 83: 16-18, November 29, 1993.

Michael Jackson gives first live interview to Oprah Winfrey [cover story]. Il. Pors. *Jet* 83: 62-63 February 8, 1993.

Michael Jackson gives revealing record breaking interview to Oprah Winfrey. *Jet* IL. Pors. 83: 56-57 March 1, 1993.

Michael Jackson tries to keep career from crumbling as he fights addiction to painkiller drugs and charges of child molestation [cover story]. A. Collier. Il. Pors. *Jet* 85: 54-59 December 6, 1993.

Michael Jackson's album soars to the top of the charts. Il. Por. *Jet* 83: 60 March 8, 1993.

Michael Jackson's mother and brother Jermaine appear on television to defend superstar. Il. *Jet* 85: 59-61 December 20, 1993.

Michael Jackson's new hue. L. D. Peden. Il. Por. *American Health* 12: 28 May 1993.

Michael's malady [Interview]. Il. Por. *People's Weekly* 39: 46 March 1, 1993.

Michael's world [Cover story]. C. McGuigan. Il. Pors. *Newsweek* 122: 34-38 September 6, 1993.

Peter pan speaks. R. Corliss. Il. Pors. *Time* 141: 66-67 February 22, 1993.

The Risks of wishing upon a star. J. Giles *Newsweek* 122: 39 September 6, *1*993.

The shield of vulnerability. J. Alter. Il. *Newsweek* 122: 38 September 6, 1993.

Superstar Michael Jackson is back and ready to fight back! Il. Por. *Jet* 85: 56-57 December 27, 1993-January 3, 1994.

Transatlantic hide and seek. J. Giles. Il. Pors. *Newsweek* 122: 70-71 November 29, 1993.

The vanishing [Cover story]. E. Gleick. Il. Pors. *People's Weekly* 40: 42-47 November 29, 1993.
We are the weird. E. Diamond. Il. Por. *New Yorker* 26: 28+ September 13, 1993.
Who's bad? R. Corliss. Il. Pors. *Time* 142: 54-56 September 6, 1993.

1994

The check is in the mail. J. Giles. Il. Por. *Newsweek* 123 p. 57 February 7, 1994.
Did Michael do it? [Cover story] M. A. Fischer. Il. Pors. *Gentleman's Quarterly* 64 pp. 214-21+ October 1994.
Dodging the bullet. [Cover story] B. Hewitt. Il. Pors. *People's Weekly* 41 pp. 64-68 February 7, 1994.
Fear of flying. P. D. Bauman. *Commonweal* 121 pp. 4-5 February 25, 1994.
Federal jury rules in favor of Michael Jackson, others charged with stealing songs. Il. Por. *Jet* 85 pp. 58-59 January 31, 1994.
Hungarian rhapsody. D. Santow. Il. Pors. *People's Weekly* 41 pp. 64-68 February 7, 1994.
A Message to Michael. P. Johnson. Il. *Essence* 24 p. 146 March 1994.
Michael and Lisa. Il. Pors. *Jet* 86 pp. 56-57, August 15, 1994.
Michael Jackson and Lisa Marie Presley 'look forward to raising a family and living happy…' [Cover story] R. E. Johnson. Il. Pors. *Jet* 86 Pp. 56-60 August 22, 1994.
Michael Jackson denies report that he wed Elvis Presley's daughter. Il. Pors. *Jet* 86 p. 59 July 25, 1994.
Michael Jackson joins family during 'Jackson family honors' gala fundraiser in Las Vegas. IL Pors. *Jet* 85 p. 54+ March 7, 1994.
Michael Jackson makes surprise appearance at NAACP Image Awards. Il. Por. *Jet* 85 pp. 58-60 January 24, 1994.
Michael Jackson owns rights to Rose Bowl champs fight song, 'On Wisconsin'. Il. Por. *Jet* 85 p. 64 January 24, 1994.

Michael Jackson settles suit, maintains innocence and "gets on with his life" [cover story] IL. Pors. *Jet* 85 pp. 58-62 February 14, 1994.

Michael Jackson speaks: "I am totally innocent of any wrongdoing'. Por. *Jet* 85 pp. 60-61 January 10, 1994.

Michael Jackson 'thankful' child molestation probe over, no charges filed but case to stay open. Il. Por. *Jet* 86 pp. 46-47 October 10, 1994.

Michael Jackson's parents Joseph and Katherine say: "LaToya is still lying – there are people trying to destroy our son. We love him" [Cover story] R. E. Johnson. Il. Pors. *Jet* 85 pp. 54-59 January 10, 1994.

Michael tells 'where I met Lisa Marie and how I proposed' [cover story] R. E. Johnson. Il. Pors. *Ebony* 4 9 pp. 118-24+ October 1994.

Neverland meets Graceland [cover story] T. Giatto. Il. Pors. *People's Weekly* 42 pp. 30-35 August 15, 1994.

Nightmare in Neverland. M. Orth. IL. Pors. *Vanity Fair* 57 Pp. 70-77+ January 1994.

The price is right. R. Corliss. Il. Por. *Time* 143 pp. 60-61 February 7, 1994.

Royal wedding. G. Belafonte. Il. Pors. *Time* 144 p. 63 August 15, 1994.

Vow? Wow! K.S. Schneider. Il. Pors. *People's Weekly* 42 pp. 160-62 July 25, 1994.

1995

Brownstone: new group makes debut on Michael Jackson's record label [cover story] IL. *Jet* 88 pp. 58-61 June 19, 1995.

Curiouser and curiouser. K. Schoemer. Il. Pors. *Newsweek* 125 p. 55 June 26, 1995.

Hooked. S. Crouch. Il. *The New Republic* 213 pp. 18-20 August 21-128, 1995.

The Jackson jive. M. Orth. IL. Pors. *Vanity Fair* No. 421 p. 114+ September 1995.

Jackson, Michael: HIStory [sound recording] Reviews *Esquire* IL. 124 p. 192 September 1995. M. Jacobson.

"OFF THE WALL SONNETS" FOR MICHAEL JACKSON

Newsweek IL. 125 p. 75 June 5, 1995. J. Giles. *Rolling Stone* IL. p. 55+ August 10, 1995. J. Hunter. *Stereo Review* IL. Por. 60, p. 90 October 1995. R. Givens. *Time* IL. Por. 145 p. 58 June 19, 1995. C. J. Farley Lazy, hazy, crazy days. J. Martin. Il. *America* 173 pp. 22-23 July 15-22, 1995. Making HIStory? J. Wiederhorn. Il. Por. *Rolling Stone* p. 24 June 15, 1995.

Michael Jackson and Sony enter joint publishing venture valued at $600 million. Por. *Jet* 89 pp. 36-37 November 27, 1995.

Michael Jackson and wife Lisa Marie Presley reveal intimate side as lovers, parents and best friends [cover story] IL. Pors. *Jet* 88 pp. 12-16, July 3, 12995.

Michael Jackson files $100 million slander suit against TV show. Por. *Jet* 87 p. 54 January 30, 1995.

Michael Jackson hosts West African ruler who made him King of Sanwi. Il. Pors. *Jet* 87 pp. 32-33 February 13, 1995.

Michael Jackson recovers after collapsing in New York. Il. Por. *Jet* 89 p. 62 December 25, 1995-January1, 1996.

Michael Jackson tells HIStory [Primetime live interview with D. Sawyer] S. Pond. Il. Pors. *TV Guide* 43 pp. 20-22 June 10-16, 1995.

A Michael Jackson thriller for Sony. R. Grover. Il. *Business Week* p. 36 July 3, 1995.

Michael Jackson Wows MTV Video Awards with show stopping performance, wind three top awards. Il. Pors. *Jet* 88 pp. 22-25, September 22, 1995.

Moments of fright. Il. Por. *People's Weekly* 44 p. 50 December 18, 1995.

The trouble with celebrity worship. F. Bruning. Il. *Maclean's* 108 p. 11 July 1171, 1995.

What, me worry? J.L. Roberts. Il. Por. *Newsweek* 126 p. 60 November 13, 1995.

"Off the Wall Sonnets" for Michael Jackson Photo. "Love, Love, Love, Love all around and over!"

1996

Citing irreconcilable differences, Lisa Marie Presley files for divorce from Michael Jackson. Pors. *Jet* 89 p. 62+ February 5, 1996.

From here to paternity. K. S. Schneider. Il. Pors. *People's Weekly* 46 pp. 48-49 November 18, 1996.

HBO: Jacko will be backo! M. hammer. Por. *TV Guide* 44 pp. 5-6 January 6-12, 1996.

Jackson, Michael and Jackson, Janet: Scream [videotape] Reviews

TCI IL. Pors. 29 pp. 52-53 November 1995.

A message to Michael. [Cover story] K. S. Schneider. Il. Pors. *People's Weekly* 45 pp. 52-56 February 5, 1996.

Michael Jackson recovering in France. Il. Por. *Jet* 89 p. 34 January 8, 1996.

Tanks for the memories: Michael Jackson imposes "HIStory" on the Czech Republic. M. Morrison. Il. Por. *Rolling Stone* p. 26 October 31, 1996.

Thinner gone bad. K. Schoemer. Il. Pors. *Newsweek* 127 pp. 48-49 January 29, 1996.

What friends are for [cover story]? K. S. Schneider. Il. Pors. *People's Weekly* 46 pp. 100-04, December 2, 1996.
When TV sold out to Michael Jackson. M. Orth. Pors. *Reader's Digest* 147 pp. 74-78 December 1995.

1997

Jacko's adventures in the Arabian Magic Kingdom. S. Macleod. Il. Por. *Time* 150 pp. 66-67 December 1, 1997.
Jackson, Michael: Blood on the Dance Floor: HIStory in the mix [sound recording] Reviews

Rolling Stone IL. Pors. P. 118 July 10-24, 1997. N. Brackett.

The king as "pop" [Cover story] D. Friend. Il. Pors. *Life* 20 pp. 92-98+ December 1997.
Michael Jackson and Wife Debbie Rowe, expecting second child, a daughter. Il. Pors. *Jet* 93 p. 31 December 22, 1997.
Michael Jackson reveals that he feels imprisoned by the paparazzi. Por. *Jet* 92 pp. 34-35, October 6, 1997.
Michael Jackson sees concert promoter in German prison; had to show ID after look-alike tried to enter. Il. Por. *Jet* 92 p. 64 May 26, 1997.

1998

Man in the Mirror. R. La Franco. Por. *Forbes* 161 p. 43-44 M arch 23, 1998.
Royal budget cuts for the king of pop. Il. Pors. *People's Weekly* 49 No. 17 pp. 6-7 May 4, 1998.
A Thriller on Wall Street [m. Jackson to issue bonds] J. L. Roberts Il. Por. *Newsweek* 132 No. 21 p. 87 November 23, 1998.

1999

The Gloved Wonder. Q. Jones. Il. Por. *Newsweek* 133 No. 26 p. 74 June 28, 1999.
Michael Jackson and wife, Debbie Rowe, agree to divorce in L.A. Il. Pors. *Jet* 97 [i.e. 96] No. 21 p. 62 October 25, 1999.
Michael Jackson talks about fame, plastic surgery and 'Thriller'. Por. *Jet* 97 No. 3 p. 57 December 20, 1999.
The once and future king [Cover story; interview] L. Bernhard. Il. Pors. *TV Guide* 47 No. 49 pp. 10-14+ December 4 -10, 1999.
Surprise! It's Over. S. Dougherty. Il. Pors *People's Weekly* 52 No. 16 pp. 73-74 October 25, 1999.

2000

Michael Jackson and Mariah Carey named best-selling artists of millennium at World Music Awards in Monaco. Por. *Jet* 97 No. 25 pp. 24-25 May 29, 2000.

2001

Children today robbed of childhood says Michael Jackson during Oxford Union address. Por. *Jet* 99 No. 15 pp. 30-31 March 26, 2001.
Michael Jackson gets all-star tribute in New York. Il. por. *Jet* 100 No. 16 pp. 56-59 October 1, 2001.
Jackson, Michael: Invincible [sound recording] Reviews
New York Por. 34 No. 45 p. 118 November 26, 2001. E. Brown.
The New Yorker IL. 77 No. 39 pp. 113-16 December 10. 2001. G. Greenman.
Newsweek Por. 139 [i.e. 138] No. 19 p. 69 November 5, 2001
Jackson, Michael: Off the wall [sound recording] Reviews
Rolling Stone Por. No. 861 p. 59 February 1, 2001.
Michael Jackson, Solomon Burke, the Flamingos inducted into Rock and Roll Hall of Fame. Por. *Jet* 99 No. 17 pp. 34-36 April 9, 2001.

Michael Jackson TV special draws 25 million viewers; 'Invincible' debuts No. 1. Por. *Jet* 100 No. 25 pp. 54-55 September 10, 2001.
The Man in the Mirror. M. Murphy and J. Graham. Por. *TV Guide* 49 No. 45 pp. 16-22, 51 November 10-16, 2001.
Higher yearning [M. Jackson's remarks before the Oxford Union Society] Por. *People's Weekly* 55 No. 11 p. 65 March 19, 2001.

2002

Black Skin, White Mask. K. R. Good. Por. *Vibe* 10 No. 3, p. 114 March 2002.
Daydream nation [MTV and America] A. Mulrine. Por. *U.S. News and World Report* 133 No. 2 p. 64 July 8-15, 2002.
Jackson heights. B. M. Raftery. Por. *Entertainment Weekly* no. 642 p. 84 March 1, 2002.
Michael Jackson Calls Music Labels Racist. Por. *Jet* 102 No. 4, p. 10 July 22, 2002.
Michael Jackson's Meltdown [Singer battles Sony] F. Goodman. Por. *Rolling Stone* No. 902, pp. 19020 August 8, 2002.
Pop Goes the King? [KM. Jackson] S. Miller. Il. Por. *People* (New York, N.Y. 2002) 58 No. 6, pp. 54-57 August 2, 2002.
Scream gem. M. A. Lipton. Por. *People's Weekly* 57 No. pp. 109-10 March 11, 2002.
Sharpton, Cochran Form Group to Protect Recording Artists; Michael Jackson Named First Member. Por. *Jet* 102 No. 2, p. 6, July 1, 2002.
Unconditional Love [Editorial] E. Wilbekin. Por. *Vibe* 10, No 3 p. 50 March 2002.
MJ; unbreakable [Cover story] R. Jones. Por. *Vibe* 10 No. 3 106-08 March 2002.
Is the King of Pop going broke? P. Wilkinson. Graph. Il. Por. *Rolling Stone* 894 pp. 25-28, April 25, 2002.

Who's the Unfairest of Them All? B. Pulley. Por. *Forbes* 170 No. 3 p. 54 August 1`2, 2002.

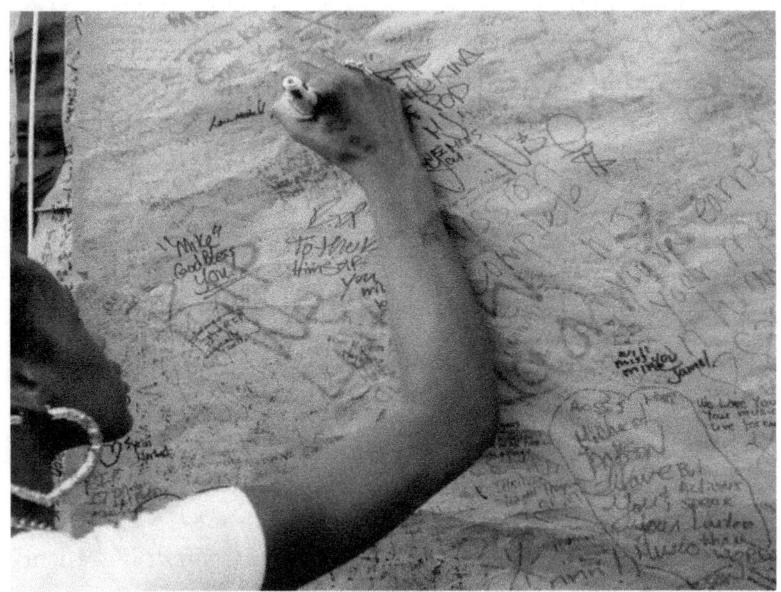

"Off the Wall Sonnets" for Michael Jackson Photo. "Go ahead, leave your loving sentiments for one who truly deserves it!"

2003

The 50 Most Intriguing Blacks of 2003. Il. *Ebony* 59 pp. 71-73, 76, 79-80, 84, 86, 88, 90, 92-94, 96-97, 101-02, 104, 106-08, 110, 112, 114, 116-17, 120, 122, 124, 126-28, 130, November 2003.

Losing His Grip [M. Jackson]. M. Orth. Por. *Vanity Fair* No. 512, p. 420-05, 443-48 April 2003.

Michael Jackson Honored In Hometown of Gary, IN; Receives Key To The City. Por. *Jet* 104 No. 1, 38-39 June 30, 2003.

Michael Jackson Honored with Germany's Bambi Award Following Baby Dangling Snafu. Por. *Jet* 102 No. 25, p. 16, 18, December 9, 2 002.

"OFF THE WALL SONNETS" FOR MICHAEL JACKSON

The President of Pop [Election of M. Jackson to presidency in a parallel universe] B. Handy and G. Sweeney. Il. Por. *Time* 161 No. 9, pp. 82 March 3, 2003.
Circus of the Star [Allegations Against M. Jackson] T. Sinclair. Il. Por. *Entertainment Weekly* No. 740 p. 12-14 December 5, 2002.
Face the Nation [M. Bashir's controversial documentary on the singer, M. Jackson] S. Dumeneco. Por. *New York* 36 no. 7, p. 16 March 3, 2003.
The King of Pop's Media Mayhem. S. Halperin. Por. *Rolling Stone* No. 918 pp. 123-14 March 20, 2003.
Michael on the Couch. D. Merkin. Por. *New York* 36, No. 43 pp. 38-39, 87 December 8, 2003.
Michael Jackson Exposed. J. Eliscu. Por. *Rolling Stone* No. 918 pp. 13-14, March 20, 2003.
The Cuffed one [Child molesting allegations against M. Jackson]. R. Corliss. Il. Por. *Time* 162 No. 22 p. 48, 50 December 1, 2003.
Fight of His Life [Child molesting allegations against M. Jackson; cover story] S. Schindehette and T. Gliatto. Il. Por. *People* (*New York, N. Y. 2002*) 60 No. 23, pp. 84-91 December 8, 2003.
From Moonwalk to Perp Walk [M. Jackson is accused of child molesting] D. J. Jefferson and A. Murr. Il. Por. *Newsweek* 142 No. 22, pp. 38-40 December 1, 2003.
Jackson's Legacy. M. Gilmore. Por. *Rolling Stone* 938-939 P. 18, December 25, 2003-January 8, 2004.
Michael Jackson Calls Child Molestation Charges 'Lies.' Por. *Jet* 104 No. 24, pp. 16-18, December 8, 2003.
Michael Jackson Ordered To Pay $5.3 million For Backing Out Of New Year's Eve Concerts. Por. *Jet* 103 No. 14 p. 20, March 31, 2003.
Our Great, Societal Neverland [Pedophilia responsibility] T. Dalrymple. *National Review* 55 No. 24, pp. 30-31, December 22, 2003.

Trouble in Neverland [Allegations against M. Jackson] J. Smolowe. Il. Por. *People* (*New York, N.Y. 2002*) 60 No. 22, pp. 58-61, December 1, 2003.

How 'Thriller' Lost Its Thrill [Coverage of M. Jackson] J. Alter. Por. *Newsweek* 142 No. 22 p. 41 December 1, 2003.

2004

Favorite Sons. E. West. Por. *Indianapolis Monthly* 28 No. 2 PP. 138-51, September, 2004.

Jackson Refutes Molestation Charges; maintains Views on Sleeping With Kids

During '60 Minutes' Interview. Por. *Jet* 105 No. 3 p. 55 January 19, 2004.

Michael Jackson [50 most intriguing blacks of 2004] Por. *Ebony* 60 No. 4 P. 90 November 2004.

Monitor [Brief news items and Obituaries] M. Kung. Il. *Entertainment Weekly* No. 764 pp. 22-23, May 7, 2004.

Passages [Short news items] O. Abel. Il. *People* (*New York, N.Y. 2002*) 62 No. 12 p. 199 September 20, 2004.

Unsolved Mysteries. Il. Por. *People* (*New York, N.Y. 2002)* 61 No. 14 pp. 141-4, 145-46 April 12, 2004.

Boswell's Life of Jackson. P. Marx. Il. *The New Yorker* 79 No. 45 pp. 34-35 February 2, 2004.

Michael Jackson [Interview] B. Rather. Por. Interview 34 no. 1 pp.92-93, 126, February, 2004.

The Truth about Michael Jackson's Money. P. Wilkinson. Por. *Rolling Stone* No. 938/939 pp. 17-18 December 25, 2003/January 8, 2004.

Et. Tu. "Nightline"? [Celebrity press coverage] J. Rosen. Por. *American*

Journalism Review 26 No. 1 pp. 18-23 February/March, 2004.

All the news that's fit. L. Dobbs. IL, *US News and World Report* 136 No. 7 p. 48 February 23/March 1, 2004.

You Don't Know Jackson. S. King. Il. *Entertainment Weekly* No. 751 p. 80 February 13, 2004.

“OFF THE WALL SONNETS” FOR MICHAEL JACKSON

Man in the Mirror. [M. Jackson] C. Ho. Coker. Por. *Essence* 34 No. 12 pp. 186-88, 190 April, 2004.

Dick Gregory Endures 40-Day Fast In Support Of Michael Jackson. Por. *Jet* 105 No. 4 p. 36, January 26, 2004.

And the verdict is .... Guilty! A. Goldman.il. *TV Guide* 52 No. 3 Pp. 51-52, 54 January 17-23, 2004.

Crime Watch. Il. Por. *People* (*New York, N.Y. 2002*) 61No. 18 p. 76 May 10, 2004.

Fired Gun. D. Dunne. Il. Por. *Vanity Fair* No. 531 pp. 178, 180, 182 November 2004.

His Story [M. Jackson] J. Smolowe. Il. Por. People (New York, N.Y. 2002) 61 No. 1 pp. 64-65, January 12, 2004.

Michael Jackson Charged in Case Stemming From Child Molestation Allegations. Por. *Jet* 105, No. 2 p. 64 January 12, 2004.

Monitor [Brief news items and obituaries] IL. *Entertainment Weekly* 770 pp. 28-29 June 18, 2004.

Monitor [Brief news items and obituaries] M. Kung. Il. *Entertainment Weekly* No. 762-763 pp., 28-29 April 30, 2004.

Monitor [Brief news items and obituaries] M. Kung. Il. *Entertainment Weekly* 768 pp. 26-27 June 4, 2004.

Monitor [Brief news items and obituaries] Mk. Kung. Il. Entertainment *Weekly* No. 769 pp. 30-31 June 11, 2004.

Monitor [Brief news items and obituaries] M. Kung and others. *Entertainment Weekly* No. 765 p. 23 May 14, 2004.

Monitor [Brief news items and obituaries] W. Pastorek. Por. *Entertainment Weekly* No. 790 p. 20 October 29, 2004.

Neverland’s Lost Boys. M. Orth. Por. *Vanity Fair* 523 pp. 384-89, 415-21 March 2004.

Newsmakers [Short news items] IL. *Newsweek* 32 No. 18 p. 67 May 3, 2004.

Notebook [Short news items and obituaries] IL. *Time* 163 No. 19 pp. 19-21, 26 May 10, 2004.

Off the Wall. J. Spong. Il. Por. Texas Monthly 32 No. 2 pp. 38, 40, 45-46 February 2004.

Passages [Short news items] T. L. Redwood. Il. *People* (*New York, N.Y. 2002*) 61 No. 16 p. 71 April 16, 2004.

Prosecutor Tried To Get Michael Jackson On Child Molestation Charges Years ago. *Jet* 104 No. 24 p. 17 December 8, 2004.

Scoop [Short news items] IL. *People* (*New York, N.Y. 2002*) 61 No. 25 pp. 19-20, 22, 24 June 28, 2004.

Star-Stricken. J. Durbin. Por. *Maclean's* 17 No. 25 56-57 June 21, 2004.

Who's in His Corner? [M. Jackson] IL. Por. People (*New York, N.Y. 2002*) 61 No. 4 pp. 44-45, February 2, 200.

"Ya Heard?" [Short news items] A. Woodson. Il. *Vibe* 12 No. 9 p 110 September 2004.

2005

Is Michael Jackson Getting a Reality Show? M. Murphy. Por. *TV Guide* 53 No. 28, p. 80 July 10-16, 2005.

The Beautiful Shall Inherit the Earth. J. M. Laskas. Il. Por. *Gentleman's Quarterly* 75 No. 5, 240-45 May 2005.

King of Pop Faces Grueling Nominations Process on Hill. Por. *Weekly Standard* 10 No. 20, p. 40 February 7, 2005.

The Fake Trial of Michael Jackson. [E! Entertainment Television presentation of M. Jackson Trial] G. Gumpert and S. J. Drucker. Por. *Television Quarterly* 35, No. 32/4 Spring/Summer 2005.

The True Believers [M. Jackson's fans] L. Ali. Il. Por. *Newsweek* 145: No. 10, 52-54, March 7, 2005.

Another Accuser's Explosive Charges. [M. Jackson trial] IL. Por. *People* (*New York, N.Y. 2002*) 64 No. 15 p. 72 April 18, 2005.

As End Nears. Who's Winning? [M. Jackson trial] J. Smolowe. Il. Por. *People* (*New York, N.Y. 2002*) 063, No. 22 p. 79-80 June 6, 2005.

Beating the Rap [M. Jackson trial] B. Hewitt. Il. Por. *People* (*New York, N.Y. 2002*) 63 No. 25, 58-61 June 27, 2005.

"OFF THE WALL SONNETS" FOR MICHAEL JACKSON

Beyond the Pale. P. J. Williams. Il. *The Nation* 280: No 20, p. 12 May 23, 2005.

C.S.I. Neverland [The Jackson trial] M. Orth. Por. *Vanity Fair* No. 539 p. 80-85, 134-37, July 2005.

The Case Against Michael Jackson [Child Molesting trial pending in California] P. Wilkinson. Il. Por. *Rolling Stone* No. 967, p. 13-14, February 10, 2005.

Celebrities Behaving Madly. D. Dunne. Il. Por. *Vanity Fair* 540, p. 86, 88, 90 August 2005.

The Gloves Come Off. [M. Jackson trial] B. Hewitt. Il. Por. *People* (*New York, N.Y. 2002*)

In the Grip of Predators. B. Amiel. Il. Por. *Maclean's* 118, No. 24, p. 4 2-4 6, June 13, 2005.

Inside the Michael Jackson Trial. M. Murphy. Il. *TV Guide* 53 No. 14, p. 13 April 3-9, 2005.

Inside the Strangest Trial on Earth [M. Jackson case] M. Taibbi. Il. Por. *Rolling Stone* 971, p. 35-36, 38, 65 April 7, 2005.

Jacko's Bad Day in Court. [Trial of M. Jackson] R. Corliss. Il. Por. *Time* 165: No. 2, p. 56-57 March 21, 2005.

Jackson vs. the State of California. Il. Por. People (*New York, N.Y. 2002*) 63: No. 6, pp. 66-67 February 14, 2005.

Jackson's Troubling Trial [Interview with J. Silberg] D. Cole. *U.S. News and World Report* 138 No. 10, p. 18, March 21, 2005.

King's Court [M. Jackson's Fans] J. Katz. Il. *Los Angeles Magazine* 50 No. 7 pp. 74-83, July 2005.

Looking for Boundaries. T. Dalrymple. Por. *National Review* 57 No. 11, pp. 26-27 June 20, 2005.

Michael Jackson Not Guilty in Molestation Trial. Il. Por. *Jet* 107, No. 26 pp. 61-65, June 27, 2005.

Monitor [Brief News Item] T. Stack. Por. *Entertainment Weekly* No. 844/845 p. 24, October 14, 2005.

The Nation in the Mirror. M. Taibbi. Il. Por. *Rolling Stone* No. 977/978 pp. 69-72 June 30-July 14, 2005.

Playing the Class Card [M. Jackson's trial] A. Murr. Por. *Newsweek145* No. 10, p. 54 March 7, 2005.

"**"Off the Wall Sonnets" for Michael Jackson Photo**. "Well, the People have Spoken!"

Star Witness: Victim or Liar? [M. Jackson trial] A. Tresniowski. Il. Por. *People* (New *York, N.Y.* 2002) 63, No. 12 pp. 89-90 March 28, 2005.
The True Believers [M. Jackson's fans] L. Ali. Il. Por. *Newsweek* 145 No. 10, pp. 52-54 March 7, 2005.

"OFF THE WALL SONNETS" FOR MICHAEL JACKSON

2006

Michael Jackson to sell Neverland Ranch. Famous Glittery Glove during Auction. Por. *Jet* 14, No. 25, p. 28 January 12, 2009.
One the Block [M. Jackson possessions up for auction] R. Dyball. Il. Por. *People* (New York, N. Y.

2007

'Can he be forgiven?' [M. Jackson] A. Wherry. Por. *McLean's* 120: No. 8, 76-78 March 5, 2007.
Michael Jackson breaks silence. Remembers Mime Marcel Marceau. J. T. Bennett. Por. *Jet* 112 No. 15 p. 32 October 15, 2007.
Michael: The Thrill is Back. [M. Jackson cover story] J.T. Bennett. Por. *Ebony* 63 No. 2 80-83, 86, 88, 90-93, December 2007.
Michael Jackson: In his own words. [Interview] B. Monroe. Por. *Ebony* 63: No. 2, 94. 96, 98-100, 104-106, 109, December 2007.

2008

Scoop [Short news items]. Il. Por. *People* (*New York, N.Y. 2002*) 70 No. 4 p. 23, 25, 26, 28, 30 July 28, 2008.
OMG They're 50! C. Tapper. Por. *People* (*New York, N.Y. 2002*) 70 No. 9 pp. 94-95 September 1, 2008.
Neverland Lost? Il. Por. *People* (*New York, N.Y. 2002*) 69 No. 10 pp. 66-67 March 17, 2008.
Thrills to come [25th anniversary edition of Thriller produced by M. Jackson and featuring K. West, Akon and Will.i.am; cover story] J.T. Bennett. Por. *Jet* 112 No. 25 pp. 58-62, December 24-31, 2007.

Come Beat It. K. Tucker. Il. *Entertainment Weekly* No. 978 pp. 64-65 February 21, 2008.

2009

Michael Jackson to sell Neverland Ranch, Famous Glittery Gove During auction. Por. *Jet* 114 No. 25 p. 28 January 12, 2009.
On the Block [M. Jackson possessions up for auction] R. Dyball. Il. Por. *People* (New York, N.Y. 2002) 71 No. 8, pp. 68-69 March 2, 2009.
Monitor [Brief News Items and Obituaries] K. Ward. Il. Por. *Entertainment Weekly* No. 1024 p. 2-21 December 5, 2008.
Avoiding the Wreck. J. Muller. Por. *Forbes* 183 No. 5 pp. 34, 37, March 16, 2009.

"Off the Wall Sonnets" for Michael Jackson Photo. Patti Labelle, extraordinary talent in her own right.

NEW YORK TIMES

1984

Books - January 28; March 14
Music – January 14, 22; February 8, 29; April 3, 5, 6, 7, 8; June 27; July 5, 6, 7, 9, 15, 20, 21, 22, 24, 29, 30; August 3, 5, 6, 7, 8; September 2; Presidential Election 1984 – June 24,

Roads – May 15; South Africa – July 13; Television – Making of 'Thriller' The (TV Program) February 2
Singer Michael Jackson gives his mother red Rolls-Royce at her birthday party, Beverly Hills, Calif. (S), May 7, II 11: 4.
Police raid string of Toronto stores to end proliferation of counterfeit Michael Jackson paraphernalia (S), July 12, III, 13: 3.

1985

Movie – July 24; 28, 31.
Music – February 27; June 12; July 17; August 16.

1986

Apparel – April 17.
Motion Pictures – Captain Eo (Movie), September 14.
Sex Crimes –July 14.

1987

Motion Pictures – Captain Eo (Movie) June 24
Music – May 17; July 22; August 29, 31; September 1, 2, 3, 10, 13, 14

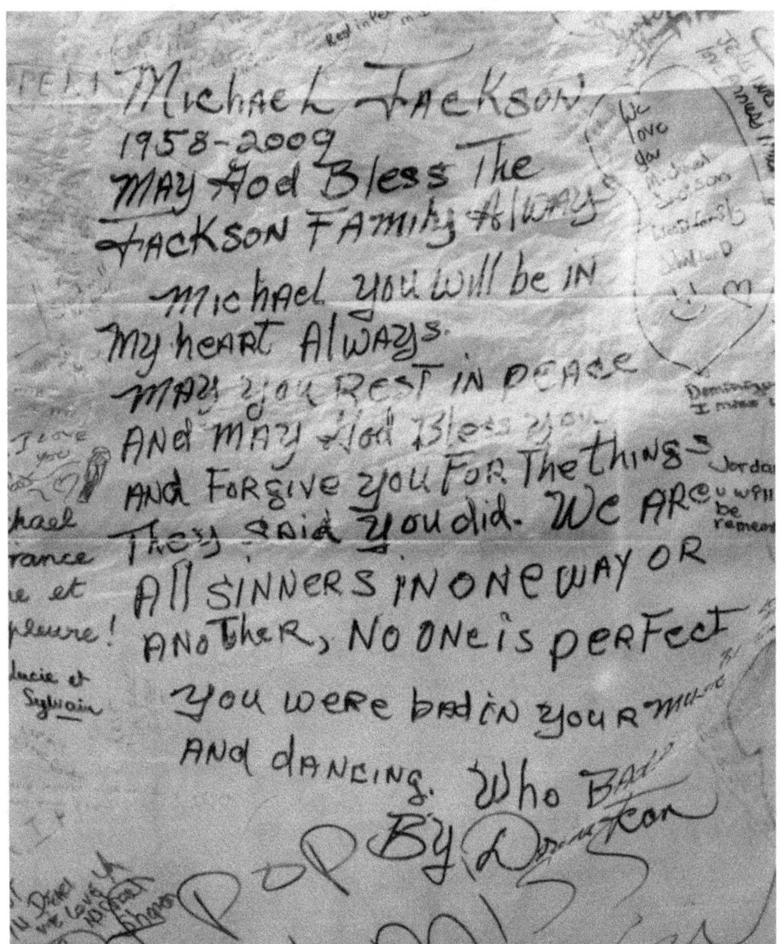

"Off the Wall Sonnets" for Michael Jackson Photo. "Sometimes they pour out the most profound sentiments that come from deep within their being, especially when it is for someone so special."

"OFF THE WALL SONNETS" FOR MICHAEL JACKSON

"Off the Wall Sonnets" for Michael Jackson Photo. Gladys Knight and the Pips and The Isley Brothers embodies The Apollo's recognition of group musical artistry flowered in talent.

1988

Book Reviews – Ken Tucker reviews Moonwalk by Michael Jackson, photo, June 5, VII, 51: 1
Dancing, March 6.
Music - January 14; February 9, 11, 24, 25; March 3, 5, 6, 23; June 29; September 12; October 11.
Scholarships and Fellowships - January 14.
Television – Motown on Showtime (TV Program), March 12; Michael Jackson Book Moonwalk, in which he discusses his show business friends, his plastic surgery, his girlfriends and his rise to musical superstardom, is about to be published by Doubleday (M), April 18: III, 22: 1.

1990

Acquired Immune Deficiency Syndrome (AIDS), April 12.
Children and Youth, April 6.
Music – November 21; December 14.

1991

Acquired Immune Deficiency Syndrome – September 21.
Music – March 21, 24, 28; November 6, 10, 17, 24, 28; December 1.
Taylor, Elizabeth – December 7.

"Off the Wall Sonnets" for Michael Jackson Photo. There is no end to the expressions of love for one so deserving as Michael Jackson.

"OFF THE WALL SONNETS" FOR MICHAEL JACKSON

1992

Music – February 4; March 16; April 25; August 13.
Shoes and Boots – September 14; November 28.

1993

Advertising – February 18; November 16.
Music – November 25.
Soft Drinks – November 15, 16
Television – March 27.
United States Politics and Government – January 18.
Oprah Winfrey will talk with Michael Jackson in 90-minute special in February; ABC says it will be Jackson's first live interview (S) - January 11, B, 7: 3.
Oprah Winfrey's interview with Michael Jackson on ABC was highest rated entertainment show in six years, (S) - February 12, C, 32: 3.
Dermatologist Arnold Klein confirms that singer Michael Jackson, his patient, suffers from vitiligo, little-understood disease which causes loss of skin pigment; photo; other doctors' comment on limited treatment available (S) - February 13, I, 7: 1.

1994

Children and Youth – April 27.
Music – February 21; September 9.
Photo of Michael Jackson accepting NAACP award for choreography, and proclaiming his innocence in face of child-molestation charges - January 7, A, 14: 4.
Los Angeles District Attorney's office reports that criminal investigation into allegations of extortion plot against Michael Jackson is completed and no action is planned (S) - January 25, A, 13: 1.

1995

Music – May 25; June 15, 16, 17, 18, 19, 22, 23, 25, 29; July 17, 20, 26, 27; September 4, 23; November 8; December 21. Thomas L. Friedman Op-Ed column on the real economic powers in the world includes singer Michael Jackson because his personal GNP is so huge (S) - May 28, IV, 121: 5.

1996

Gary (Indiana) - November 29.
King Entertainment - March 20.
Landmark Entertainment Group – October 30.
Music – February 11; May 9; October 7; November 25. Lisa Marie Presley and Michael Jackson are planning to divorce; their photos (M), January 19, B, 5: 1.
Lisa Marie Presley files for divorce from Michael Jackson; photo (S), January 21, IV, 2: 1.
Michael Jackson weds Debbie Rowe in Australia; Jackson says Rowe is six months pregnant with their child (S) November 15, B, 7: 1.

"Off the Wall Sonnets" for Michael Jackson Photo. Maestro, who composed across the wide spat of musical genre and had been instrumental in much of Michael Jackson's resounding creative success.

"OFF THE WALL SONNETS" FOR MICHAEL JACKSON

1997

Boxing – December 16.
Music – January 6; May 20; June 23; September 7.
Michael Jackson and Debbie Rowe have a baby girl – February 14, B: 6: 1.
Michael Jackson was made a Member of Bafokengka Bakwena (People of the Crocodile) Tribe of Phokeng, South Africa – October 14, B 12: 6.

1998

Africa – July 7.
Amusement Parks March - 19.
Apparel February - 27.

2000

Music – January 9; February 24; December 21.

2001

Art – April 20.
Blacks – September 2.
Israel – March 23.
Music – March 20; September7, 10, 13; October 28; November 1; December 20.
Terrorism – September 18.

2002

Music – June 6, 15; July 7, 8, 10, 11, 15, 16; October 7; November 22, 23.

"Off the Wall Sonnets" for Michael Jackson Photo. These sonnets are certainly "Living Off the Wall!"

"Off the Wall Sonnets" for Michael Jackson Photo. Chaka Khan, Musical Genius who ruled the dance floor.

"OFF THE WALL SONNETS" FOR MICHAEL JACKSON

"Off the Wall Sonnets" for Michael Jackson Photo. This is quite a collection of a young genius coming of age to ultimately excel!"

"Off the Wall Sonnets" for Michael Jackson Photo. More of the throngs of fans who came fore Michael!

"Off the Wall Sonnets" for Michael Jackson Photo. Michael, as clear as day!"

"OFF THE WALL SONNETS" FOR MICHAEL JACKSON

"Off the Wall Sonnets" for Michael Jackson Photo. Classic Michael Jackson pose with fan sentiments written all over.

2004

Acquired Immune Deficiency Syndrome -, April 1.
Housing - May 7.
Motion Pictures – Miss Cast Away (Movie), May 31.
Music – January 4; February 12; October 24.

Sex Crimes – January 1, 3, 4, 5, 17, 21, 25; February 3, 12, 14; April 3, 14, 22, 23, 24, 26, 27; May 1, 6, 9, 29; June 26; July 15, 23, 28; August 15, 17; September 3, 4, 18; October 13, 24; December 6, 21.
Television – Man in the Mirror: The Michael Jackson Story (TV Program), August 6.
Transit Systems, January 18.

Music - May 25; June 15, 16, 17, 18, 19, 22, 23, 25, 29; July 17, 20, 26, 27; September 4, 23; November 8; December 21.

2005

Housing - June 19.
Music - May 5, June 14, 15, July 12, September 14, November 25.
Sex Crimes - January 13, 14, 15, 29, 31; February 1, 6, 10, 15, 16, 29, 22, 23, 24, 25, 28; March 1, 2, 3, 4, 5, 8, 9, 10, 11, 12, 15, 16, 17, 18, 19, 22, 23, 24, 26, 27, 29, 30, 31; April 2, 5, 6, 8, 9, 11, 12, 13, 14, 17, 18, 20, 24, 25, 26, 27, 28, 29, 30; May 4, 5, 6, 7, 10, 11, 12, 13, 14, 17, 18, 20, 24, 25, 26, 27, 28; June 1, 2, 3, 4, 6, 7, 8, 9, 12, 14, 15, 16; August 9, 24, 31; December 11.

"Off the Wall Sonnets" for Michael Jackson Photo. Celia Cruz, that "Forgiving is not forgetting" Spanish songbird and extraordinary talent.

"OFF THE WALL SONNETS" FOR MICHAEL JACKSON

"Off the Wall Sonnets" for Michael Jackson Photo. "Having made the **Cover of Ebony Magazine**, then you have arrived!" And "How peaceful young Michael looks before stardom in a life of creativity, composing and competitive negotiations for concerts!"

"I urge all young people to go for their dreams. If they do, many of the world's problems will be solved." **Michael Jackson**

22. MICHAEL JACKSON ON TV: A CREATIVE COMPOSER, SONGWRITER AND HUMAN BEING EXTRAORDINAIRE

Jun 25, 2009, 08:31 PM | by Ken Tucker
Categories: Music, News, Television

Michael Jackson altered American entertainment with his appearance on the 1983 *Motown 25: Yesterday, Today, Forever* TV special. Coming at a time when Jackson was chafing to establish himself once and for all as a solo artist separate from the brother-act the Jackson 5, he made the boldest move of his career in front of a live studio audience.

Singing his hit "Billie Jean," he flashed the moves that became known as the Moonwalk. It's difficult to remember now, after decades of pop and hip-hop acts having copied Jackson's choreography, how astounding a spectacle this was. The man was ... moving backward while walking forward. He was updating Gene Kelly dance-steps to a rhythm-and-blues song and adding his own slinky-robotic twist to them. After this, pop-music dance would never be the same:

Jackson made a series of music videos that featured endlessly creative variations on the *Motown 25* choreography. It didn't matter whether he worked in long-form (with director John Landis on the "Thriller" monster-mash video) or short (the dazzling dance-work on songs that weren't even top-tier Jackson songs, such as "The Way You Make Me Feel" and "Smooth Criminal").

"OFF THE WALL SONNETS" FOR MICHAEL JACKSON

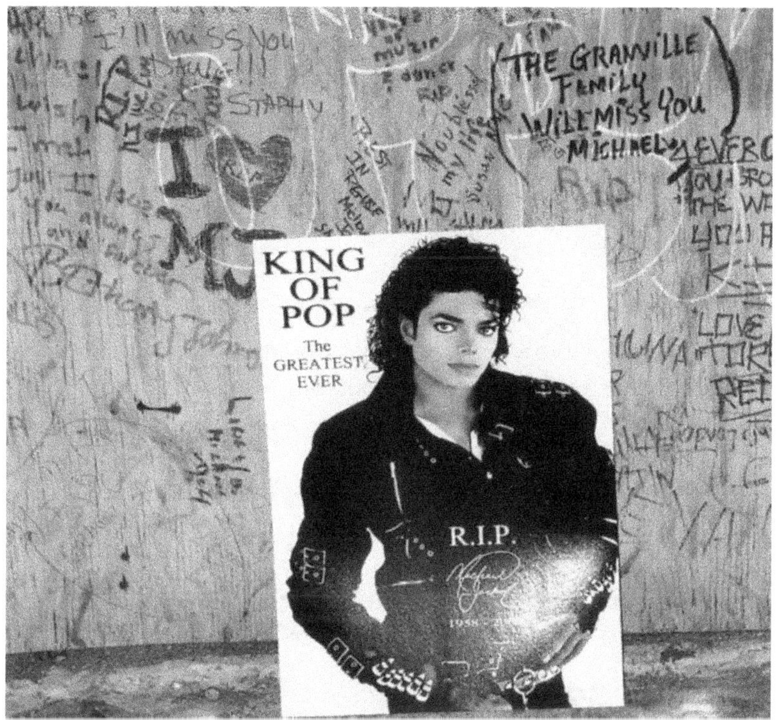

"Off the Wall Sonnets" for Michael Jackson Photo. Well, there's the **King of Pop**!"

Jackson's videos had an importance beyond their own existence: They helped break down the barrier that kept R&B videos from being shown on MTV, which originally had a rock-only orientation.

When it came to TV, Jackson in later life did not benefit from the medium. His TV interviews after he became a reclusive, more eccentric man, such as the 2003 ABC special *Living With Michael Jackson*, did him no favors in reestablishing him as a mass-audience favorite.

But those early and mid-career TV appearances capture what we should remember most about Jackson: that he was an artist who was both very much in the tradition of great pop, rock, and soul legends, and a revolutionary figure who broke new ground.

Michael Jackson: Friends and colleagues mourn the entertainer Jun 25, 2009, 08:08 PM | by Entertainment Weekly Categories: Legacy, Music, News

Hours after Michael Jackson's sudden death from cardiac arrest June 25, stunned friends and family responded with shock and grief.

LISA MARIE PRESLEY (who was married to Jackson from 1994 to 1996) "I am completely shocked and saddened by Michael's death. My heart goes out to his children and his family."

ELIZABETH TAYLOR "Oh God! I'm going to miss him. I can't yet imagine life without him. But I guess with God's help... I'll learn. I keep looking at the photo he gave me of himself, which says, 'To my true love Elizabeth, I love you forever.' And, I will love HIM forever."

MARTIN SCORSESE (director of the "Bad" video) "Michael Jackson was extraordinary. When we worked together on "Bad," I was in awe of his absolute mastery of movement on the one hand, and of the music on the other. Every step he took was absolutely precise and fluid at the same time. It was like watching quicksilver in motion. He was wonderful to work with, an absolute professional at all times, and -- it really goes without saying -- a true artist. It will be a while before I can get used to the idea that he's no longer with us."

MADONNA (Jackson's date to the 1991 Academy Awards, in an exclusive statement to People) "I can't stop crying over the sad news. I have always admired Michael Jackson. The world has lost one of the greats, but his music will live on forever! My heart goes out to his three children and other members of his family. God bless."

"OFF THE WALL SONNETS" FOR MICHAEL JACKSON

BRITNEY SPEARS "I was so excited to see his show in London. We were going to be on tour in Europe at the same time and I was going to fly in to see him. He has been an inspiration throughout my entire life and I'm devastated he's gone."

USHER --- "This loss has deeply saddened me. It is with a heavy heart I composed this statement. May God cover you Michael. We all lift your name up in prayer. I pray for the entire Jackson family, particularly Michael's mother, children, and all his fans that loved him so much.... I have great admiration and respect for him and I'm so thankful I had the opportunity to meet and perform with such a great entertainer, who in so many ways, transcended the culture. He broke barriers, he changed radio formats. With music, he made it possible for people like Oprah Winfrey and Barack Obama to impact the mainstream world. His legacy is unparalleled. Michael Jackson will never be forgotten."

PAUL MCCARTNEY "I feel privileged to have hung out and worked with Michael. He was a massively talented boy man with a gentle soul. His music will be remembered forever and my memories of our time together will be happy ones. I send my deepest sympathy to his mother and the whole family and to his countless fans all around the world."

SHERYL CROW (a former backup singer for Jackson) "I can't say how grateful I am, especially now, that I had the opportunity to observe his greatness every single night. Because every night he really was truly an incredible performer."

KRIS ALLEN "If you are a music fan, you are a Michael Jackson fan. Because he covered it all. He did his own thing, but it appealed to everyone -- little kids, my parents. He knew how to make everyone happy."

FERGIE “We have lost one of the greatest icons of all time. He forever set the bar for entertainers all around the world.”

NAOMI CAMPBELL (friend and costar for Jackson’s “In the Closet” video) “No artist has connected to their audience like Michael, and no one will ever be able to match what he has achieved. He gave back to people through his charity work and was an amazing father and human being. Michael touched people of every race, nationality, age and was the first truly global superstar. He is one of the all-time greats and his role in popular culture will never be surpassed and never ever be forgotten.

“Off the Wall Sonnets” for Michael Jackson Photo. “Young and Old, they keep coming to pay tribute to their idol.”

COREY FELDMAN “It is with great sadness that I acknowledge the loss of the greatest entertainer in the history of mankind. For me, he was more than that, Michael Jackson was a role model, he was someone to cry to when my childhood was unbearable, he was a brother, and he was a dear friend. I treasure the good times we shared and the inspiration that he was to me and to the world. My deepest sympathy goes out to his family, friends and fans."

EDDIE VAN HALEN "I am really shocked and deeply saddened, as I am sure the world is, to hear the news. I had the pleasure of working with Michael on "Beat It" back in '83, one of my fondest memories in my career. Michael will be missed and may he rest in peace."

BROOKE SHIELDS (who briefly dated the singer) "My heart is overcome with sadness for the devastating loss of my true friend Michael. He was an extraordinary friend, artist and contributor to the world. I join his family and his fans in celebrating his incredible life and mourning his untimely passing."

DIANA ROSS (co-star in *The Wiz*) "I can't stop crying, this is too sudden and shocking. I am unable to imagine this. My heart is hurting. I am in prayer for his kids and thc family."

WILL.I.AM (who was working with Jackson on his long-anticipated comeback album) "I am so grateful to have worked with the King. He was a gift to the world. He is a bright light and I wouldn't be surprised if the world stopped spinning tomorrow."

JANET JACKSON (statement from her manager, Kenneth Crear) "Janet Jackson is grief-stricken and devastated at the sudden loss of her brother. She is in pre-production on a film and is flying immediately to California to be with her family."

JUSTIN TIMBERLAKE "I can't find the words right now to express how deeply saddened I am by Michael's passing. We have lost a genius and a true ambassador of not only Pop music, but of all music. He has been an inspiration to multiple generations, and I will always cherish the moments I shared with him on stage and all-of the things I learned about music from him and the time we spent together. My heart goes out to his family and loved ones."

QUINCY JONES (friend and producer) "I am absolutely devastated at this tragic and unexpected news. For Michael to be taken away from us so suddenly at such a young age, I just don't have the words. Divinity brought our souls together on *The Wiz* and allowed us to do what we were able to throughout the '80s. To this day, the music we created together on *Off The Wall*, *Thriller*, and *Bad* is played in every corner of the world and the reason for that is because he had it all…talent, grace, professionalism, and dedication. He was the consummate entertainer and his contributions and legacy will be felt upon the world forever. I've lost my little brother today, and part of my soul has gone with him."

R. KELLY (who wrote Jackson's "You Are Not Alone") "I am truly saddened that my mentor, brother, and friend will no longer be with us physically. At the same time, I feel so blessed to have been touched by his music, his dance, his lyrics, and his pure genius. It is because of Michael's yesterday that I am who I am today!"

JAMIE FOXX (to *Extra*) "[I saw] him in concert in 1983, the Victory concert with his brothers. To watch people faint in the audience -- grown men fainting, women fainting -- just because he was that dynamic.... All you can say is that you hope we put our arms around his family. So much turmoil toward the end of his career...and I think that's the only thing that you can really hope for is that there is finally peace."

DIDDY "Michael Jackson showed me that you can-actually see the beat. He made the music come to life! He made me believe in magic. I will miss him!"

"OFF THE WALL SONNETS" FOR MICHAEL JACKSON

LIZA MINNELLI (longtime friend, to *The Early Show*) "I'm sure when the autopsy comes, all hell's going to break loose. So, thank God, we're celebrating him now."

HUEY LEWIS (who sang on "We Are The World") "What can be said about the guy? Super talented, and super fabulous, and super sweet at the same time. It's a sad day for all of us."

"Off the Wall Sonnets" for Michael Jackson Photo. Part of the groundswell of people congregating in the Michael Jackson Memorial environment in the Apollo vicinity.

ASHLEE SIMPSON "His death is a shock. I grew up being inspired by Michael Jackson's music and magic. He is a legend and his music and heart will forever inspire."

NE-YO "Michael Jackson will live forever through the thing that he put all of his life energy into: his music. I will do my part to keep the melody alive, to keep the energy forever changing form, but never ever dying! Long live Michael Jackson."

JC CHASEZ "Words can't begin to describe my sadness for the loss of Michael Jackson. I was honored and humbled to have the opportunity to perform with him several times and he had a profound influence on my career. Michael forever changed the world of music and entertainment, and I will always remember him for his kind and sweet spirit."

PETE WENTZ (whose band, Fall Out Boy, covered "Beat It") "Michael Jackson has been a part of my life for as long I have heard music. He, in my mind, is the ultimate entertainer of our generation. I can remember exact moments of my life based on Michael Jackson songs and videos."

JOHN LANDIS (director of "Thriller," who sued Jackson over the video earlier this year) "I was lucky enough to know and work with Michael Jackson in his prime. Michael was an extraordinary talent and a truly great international star. He had a troubled and complicated life and despite his gifts, remains a tragic figure. My wife Deborah and I will always have great affection for him."

DON CORNELIUS (longtime *Soul Train* host) "I met Michael Jackson at the age of eight -- when his father and my new friend Joe Jackson first began to bring the Jackson 5 to Chicago, from their home in Gary, Indiana, for concert appearances. As the word of the Jackson 5's devastating abilities as concert artists had already begun to spread like an out-of-control forest fire.... Michael Jackson's... amazing power as an entertainer was clear and unmistakable; and has never slowed to this very day! His passing will be grieved far beyond that of any other singer, composer, producer, dancer, and choreographer, in the history of the world.

"OFF THE WALL SONNETS" FOR MICHAEL JACKSON

"Off the Wall Sonnets" for Michael Jackson Photo. Lionel Richie, the artiste who could go "All Night Long!"

BERRY GORDY (Motown Records producer and founder, via CNN) "I am somewhat numb. I'm shocked at the death of Michael Jackson. It's like a dream, a bad dream. He was so much like a son to me. It's just hard to realize that Michael Jackson is not here.... As a kid Michael was always beyond his years, he was an innovator, he was a genius at what he did. He had a knowingness about him. At 9 years old, when I first started working with him, he seemed to me like he had been here before. He was just so knowledgeable about life."

WHITNEY HOUSTON (via CNN) "I am full of grief."

"Off the Wall Sonnets" for Michael Jackson Photo.

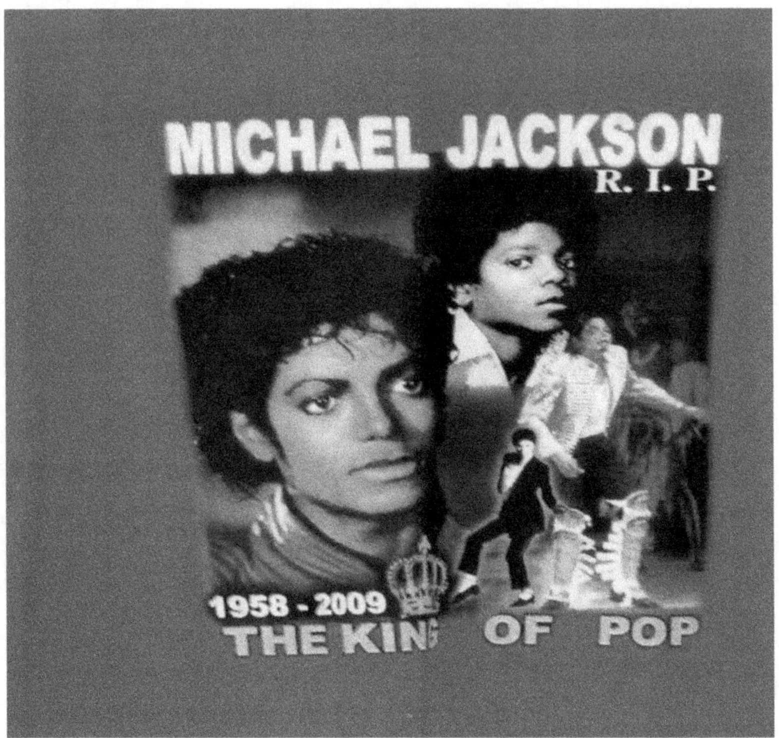

"Off the Wall Sonnets" for Michael Jackson Photo. "The King of Pop Music!"

MARIAH CAREY (via CNN) "I am heartbroken. My prayers go out to the Jackson family, and my heart goes out to his children. Let us remember him for his unparalleled contribution to the world of music, his generosity of spirit in his quest to heal the world, and the joy he brought to his millions of devoted fans throughout the world. I feel blessed to have performed with him several times and to call him my friend. No artist will ever take his place. His star will shine forever."

JOHN LEGEND (via CNN) "Michael Jackson will always be remembered as one of the greatest performers in the history of popular music. As a child of the '80s, I feel as though his music and his videos have been an inseparable part of my life and that of an entire generation. And the powerful thing about great music is that it will always live on. He was and always will be an icon. My heart goes out to his family, friends and countless fans for their tragic loss."

RUSSELL SIMMONS (via CNN) "Michael Jackson was my generation's most iconic cultural hero. Courageous, unique and incredibly talented. He'll be missed greatly."

DICK CLARK (via CNN) "I knew Michael as a child and watched him grow over the years. Of all the thousands of entertainers I have worked with, Michael was THE most outstanding. Many have tried and will try to copy him, but his talent will never be matched. He was truly one-of-a-kind."

CELINE DION (via CNN) "I am so devastated by this terrible news. From the beginning of my career, he was my idol in show business. He was a genius and an incredible artist! I remember when I was growing up and watching him on TV, and all his videos...I had his poster on my wall...he was so amazing...his singing, his writing, his dancing.... It's unbelievable that he's no longer with us."

REV. AL SHARPTON (via CNN) "A friend of Michael's for the last 35 years, I call on people around the world to pray for him and his family in the hour. I have known Michael since we were both teens, worked with him, marched for him, hosted him at our House of Justice headquarters in New York, and we joined together to eulogize our mutual idol, James Brown. I have known him at his high moments and his low moments and I know he would want us to pray for his family."

WYCLEF JEAN (via CNN) "Michael Jackson was my musical god. He made me believe that all things are possible, and through real and positive music, he can live forever! I love Michael Jackson. God bless him."

GLORIA ESTEFAN (via CNN) "The two great losses that we have felt today can only be balanced by the beautiful things that they left behind in our world. Farrah Fawcett and Michael Jackson will live forever in my heart as unforgettable and eternal."

DEEPAK CHOPRA "Michael Jackson will be remembered, most likely, as a shattered icon, a pop genius who wound up a mutant of fame. That's not who I will remember, however. His mixture of mystery, isolation, indulgence, overwhelming global fame, and personal loneliness was intimately known to me. For twenty years I observed every aspect, and as easy as it was to love Michael -- and to want to protect him -- his sudden death yesterday seemed almost fated."

CHRIS CORNELL (who wrote the rendition of "Billie Jean" that David Cook performed on *American Idol*) "I remembered being six years old and seeing the Jackson 5 on our black and white TV. His brothers were cool but he had a halo around him. Superstar at 12. What promise. He had magic...! He was amazingly talented and largely misunderstood. I hope that the media will be kind and celebrate the genius instead of cashing in on the tabloid angles that made him a prisoner. I think he deserves that."

CAROLE BAYER SAGER (Jackson's Invincible was dedicated to the songwriter) "He was one of, if not THE greatest entertainer of all time, and was without question the 'King of Pop.' He was also my friend. He recorded a song of mine on his 1979 *Off The Wall* album and in 1981 we sang a duet together. We spent a considerable amount of time together in 2001 at my home music studio and I saw him in a totally different light -- as a nurturing and caring father. I was so honored that he dedicated that album to me. My heart and prayers are with his family, his three children, my friend

Elizabeth Taylor, and all of us who are mourning the premature loss of his very precious life."

"Off the Wall Sonnets" for Michael Jackson Photo. Michael so relished his fans, supporters, admirers and Impersonators.

"Off the Wall Sonnets" for Michael Jackson Photo. Prince, "The Purple Rain" artiste who knew, "When Doves Cry!"

"Off the Wall Sonnets" for Michael Jackson Photo. Smokey Robinson, an early Motown talent from the Jackson 5's beginnings, a creative music legend.

"OFF THE WALL SONNETS" FOR MICHAEL JACKSON

"Off the Wall Sonnets" for Michael Jackson Photo. The throngs gather at the Apollo Theater in respectful honor of a multi-talented angelic spirit, humanitarian and figure well-liked and respected worldwide.

"Off the Wall Sonnets" for Michael Jackson Photo. Delivering the classic image of Michael.

"OFF THE WALL SONNETS" FOR MICHAEL JACKSON

"Off the Wall Sonnets" for Michael Jackson Photo. "Look at the King, the King, the King!"

"Off the Wall Sonnets" for Michael Jackson Photo. "It is FAN-tastic!"

"OFF THE WALL SONNETS" FOR MICHAEL JACKSON

"Off the Wall Sonnets" for Michael Jackson Photo. Young Impersonators Abound!

"Off the Wall Sonnets" for Michael Jackson Photo.

Off the Wall Sonnets" for Michael Jackson Photo. Young Impersonator strikes a Pose!

"OFF THE WALL SONNETS" FOR MICHAEL JACKSON

"Off the Wall Sonnets" for Michael Jackson Photo.

www.ingramcontent.com/pod-product-compliance
Lightning Source LLC
LaVergne TN
LVHW010612100826
845148LV00014B/2935